CONTEMPORARY ISSUES

RACISM AND ETHNIC DISCRIMINATION

ALANA LENTIN

ROSEN
PUBLISHING®

New York

For Partho

This edition published in 2011 by:

The Rosen Publishing Group, Inc.
29 East 21st Street
New York, NY 10010

Library of Congress Cataloging-in-Publication Data

Lentin, Alana.
Racism and ethnic discrimination / Alana Lentin.
    p. cm.—(Contemporary issues)
Includes bibliographical references and index.
ISBN 978-1-4488-1861-7 (library binding)
1. Racism—Juvenile literature. 2. Race discrimination—Juvenile literature. I. Title.
HT1521.L4125 2011
305.8—dc22

                                                                2010028604

Manufactured in the United States of America

CPSIA Compliance Information: Batch #W11YA: For further information, contact Rosen Publishing, New York, New York, at 1-800-237-9932.

Originally published in 2008 as part of the Oneworld Beginner's Guides series. Copyright © Alana Lentin 2008

Contents

Acknowledgments

Grateful thanks go firstly to Louis Lentin whose comments from a lay reader's point of view helped keep me on my toes! I would also like to thank Marsha Filion at Oneworld Publications for thinking of me for this project and for her insightful and practical approach to the editing process.

Introduction

Enter "racism" into Google and you will be informed that about thirty million Web sites contain the word. If nothing else, this piece of trivia tells us that racism is alive and well and probably here to stay. If so many pages on the Internet can be filled by the subject, one would be right in asking how a short book like *Racism and Ethnic Discrimination* could even start to cover adequately the subject of racism.

Nonetheless, racism is a subject that most people – in Western societies at least – seem to have an opinion on. Everyday conversations can contain references to racism that can leave us perplexed as to what it really means. The French sociologist, Michel Wieviorka, noted that it is commonplace to hear talk of "anti-youth racism," or "anti-worker racism." So, is racism just anything that discriminates? Apparently not, because when probed further, racism provokes a "don't go there" attitude that reveals that it is something we are both deeply familiar with and profoundly troubled by. But do we really know why?

The purpose of this book is to go beyond commonsense or gut feeling reactions to racism that imply that we know all we need to know about it. It aims to reveal the complexity and heterogeneity of racism from its historical, theoretical, contemporary sociological, and – most importantly – political dimensions. Yet this will be done in a straightforward way that demystifies rather than complicates this perpetually thorny issue.

While it is more and more common to hear that racism is as old as civilization and that no society has been free of it, this book will be based on the argument that the origins of racism are to be found in Europe, in the modern era. This setting of racism in place and time is important because, as the late British sociologist Ivan Hannaford (1996: 4), reminds us:

> In the modern world we have become so accustomed to thinking within
> a framework of race and ethnicity that we are quite unable to conceive
> of a past that may not have had this framework.

My argument in this book is that, besides being historically inaccurate, seeing racism as perennial is not conducive to imagining a future without it. This should be the aim of those interested in deepening their knowledge of the origins and functions of racism. In addition, by demonstrating how racism developed since the Enlightenment and with the advance of modern nation-state building, I reveal how and why racism continues to be such an important factor in society today.

Isn't racism natural?

When we ask why racism is apparently still so important, despite the end of colonialism, slavery, and the Holocaust, frequently the answer comes back: "It's natural, isn't it?," followed often by references to the "survival of the fittest" and "natural selection." The success and longevity of Social Darwinism – the extrapolation of Charles Darwin's theories on animal behavior and their application to human societies – astounds. It also reveals the degree to which the legacy of the racial theory of the nineteenth century is hardwired into our knowledge.

For many, the naturalness, or primordiality, of racism is as obvious as its permanence in time. This is linked to the way in which the word "racism" has entered into everyday speech and, therefore, our consciousnesses. The idea of racism is so widespread that we easily mistake it for something that is just there: a fact of life. Racism is associated in this way to the fear and even hatred that human beings are commonly expected to have of each other.

A story told to me by a mother who claimed that her child was scared of black men illustrates this. This intrigued me because the mother and child are both black themselves. On enquiring further I learned that the toddler had once been frightened by his grandfather, an African man with a gruff deep voice. Being the child of a single mother, he was unused to seeing men and hearing male voices. The story demonstrates how attitudes are learned through interaction with society and disproves the commonsense idea that racism is a natural human reaction. However, if I had not questioned my colleague further, I may have been left with the impression that fear based on racism is inherent and that, therefore, there is no need to ask why it exists or what causes it to persist.

Just how mistaken this is can be seen in the solutions that have been commonly proposed to racism since the end of the Second World War and the discovery of the horrors in which racism, taken to its extremes, can result: the Nazi genocide of millions of Jews, Gypsies, homosexuals, and others. Advisers to governments and international institutions, such as the United Nations, who made proposals for combating racism, generally explained it in pathological terms. Racism was seen as an individual problem, arising either from delusions, akin to those associated with madness, or ignorance. According to this logic, the Holocaust could be explained in large part by the personal fanaticism of Adolf Hitler. Racism could be solved by increasing our knowledge of "other cultures."

Both the identification of the problem and the proposed solution suppose that racism is essentially apolitical. It is likened to a disease that inexplicably spreads from the individual mind to attack unwitting societies. This is clearly an unsatisfactory explanation, belied by the fact that racism continues to play such an important role in Western societies, despite decades of post-colonialism and immigration leading to the multicultural societies in which almost all of us live. Getting to know people from other cultures, although clearly beneficial, has proven to be insufficient for ending racist discrimination.

Too much diversity?

The common answer to this evident problem, which is met with increasing support in mainstream commentary, is that it is precisely the fact of living together in culturally diverse societies that leads to the persistence of racism. Whereas this was once an opinion expressed only by far right-wing political parties, it has gained in acceptance over recent years. For example, as is discussed in Chapter 5, David Goodhart, the editor of the magazine *Prospect*, wrote in 2004 that too much diversity has led to a decrease in social cohesion in advanced modern societies. Similar claims have been made in countries such as Australia, the US, and the Netherlands, where multiculturalism and diversity have been blamed for problems such as crime and violence, segregation and terrorism.

In opposition to these attacks on multiculturalism that ultimately blame the victims of racism, I shall seek to draw out the complexities of racism that this type of finger-pointing masks. Throughout, this book opposes the idea that racism, both today and in the past, is the result of a natural inclination of human beings to fear or hate others they consider different to them, an idea that is growing with an increase in the diversity of our populations.

The politics of racism

Racism and Ethnic Discrimination is centered on the basic principle that racism is inherently political. It thus relies on particular political conditions in order to function. The expression "to play the race card" acknowledges the well-documented tendency of political parties across the spectrum to use arguments about race to win votes. However, what I am arguing here goes further than the mere harnessing of racism to particular political purposes at various moments. Focusing too much on the "race card" would suggest that racism is sporadic, to be used and discarded like a prop. On the contrary, racism is political in the sense that it has become inherent in the structures of our political apparatus: the nation-state. Racism emerges and becomes increasingly important in parallel to and in relation to the development of nation-states in Europe.

Racism, in other words, needs a context in which to become relevant. The French philosopher Etienne Balibar has argued that there is a relationship of "reciprocal determination" between racism and nationalism. Racism cannot be reduced to nationalism, or vice versa, yet each aids and abets the other. By the mid-nineteenth century, nationalism had emerged as the dominant political ideology and led to the construction of territorial and cultural nation-states. Therefore, it is the nation-state that is the main political vehicle for racism. To explain this, I focus on the origins of racism and how it became harnessed to the particular political developments of the modern era that lead to the modern state system as we know it today. Racism cannot be understood without a parallel understanding of how and why we have come to live as citizens of defined states, based on the idea of a common ethnic and political heritage, territorially bound by legal frontiers and with limited membership.

Much of the book is dedicated to showing how racism is intertwined with issues such as national identity and living together in diverse societies, and the politics of immigration or the effects of legally divid-ing between "insiders"and "outsiders." It makes direct connections be-tween the history of racism and nationalism and contemporary debates about immigration and asylum, multiculturalism and social cohesion, Islamophobia and the "war on terror." The aim is to demonstrate the inherently political nature of racism as well as its ability to adapt itself to changing political, social, and economic circumstances. As Neil Macmaster (2001: 2) reminds us:

> Racism is always a dynamic process, a set of beliefs and practices that is embedded in a particular historical context, a particular social formation, and is thus continuously undergoing change, a plastic or chameleon-like phenomenon which constantly finds new forms of political, social, cul-tural or linguistic expression.

The challenge for those interested in understanding racism is to conceive of how its malleability as an idea allows it to appear as both a natural and a non-political phenomenon when it is, in fact, the contrary. The key to this is to look firstly at the idea of race itself. It is important to distinguish between race and racism because it is still common today for the term "race" to be used to define different human groups. That is not to say that race should be banished from the lexicon. Nevertheless, race cannot be used unproblematically. We can only refer to race in full recognition of the fact that it remains a salient term only because *racism* continues to exist. Despite the agreement among most social scientists that race is a social construct that has no scientific value, it persists because of the po-litical power of racism and the fact that, despite proclamations to the con-trary, it has become institutionalized in the structures of our societies.

Referring to race in descriptive terms can only be of value if it takes account of *racialization*. Racialization is the process through which the supposed inferiority of black, colonized, non-whites, and non-Western people is constructed. Today, the idea of xeno-racism describes the fact that, in the post-Communist era, racism against white, Eastern European immigrants in the West follows the same patterns of racialization. Today's global racism divides the rich and the poor worlds and is no longer a simple black-and-white issue.

Racialization involves endowing the characteristics, appearances, traditions, and lifestyles attributed to groups of different "others" with negative signifiers that are deemed to be natural and insurmountable. The development of a racialized discourse about a group of people provides justification for their discrimination. It puts into words the very thing about a particular group that is said to disturb us and pose a threat to our way of life. A clear contemporary example of the way racialization operates is the response to the attacks of September 11, 2001, and other acts of "Islamist terrorism." The attacks of 9/11 have etched the impression on our minds that there is something particular about Muslims and/or Arabs that makes them capable of carrying out such acts. The association of Arabs and Muslims with threats against our personal security is the lynchpin of Islamophobia. The paranoia and fear caused by the image of the "Muslim terrorist" mirrors the antisemitism of 1930s Europe that saw Jews as responsible for the economic and political problems that plagued the continent.

The fact that racialization and racism are repeated, affecting different groups over time, does not mean that racism is inevitable. Rather, it shows that considerable transformations of our political systems, our social and cultural infrastructure, and our discourse – the very way in which language is used – needs to change if racism in Western societies is to be overcome.

Theory and practice

Each of the book's chapters deals with a specific factor in the analysis of racism, always relating it to the political dimension that underpins the discussion as a whole. Chapter 1 deals with the origins of the idea of race, from racial science to the marriage with the politics of nationalism, and historically as a specifically European phenomenon. In Chapter 2, the experience of racism within the particular context of colonialism is dealt with. This is connected to the processes of racialization and how these impact on the daily lives of the people whom racism affects.

Chapter 3 examines the case of antisemitism. Antisemitism, and in particular the tragic events of the Nazi Holocaust, are often held up as the example of racism par excellence. This can be misleading because it means that racism in other circumstances can be overlooked or denied. On the contrary, the case of antisemitism serves to exemplify how racism in general works and, in particular, how it can shape both society and politics.

In Chapter 4 we fast-forward to the present day and debate the idea that we are living in a post-racial age. Theories of the new racism, which focus on culture rather than biology, have been used to infer that "real racism" is a thing of the past. The cases of antisemitism and Islamophobia reveal how both culture and biology have been used interchangeably in the construction of racist arguments. Yet it is too early to discount biological racism: work in genetics on "human genome diversity" demonstrates that race still influences scientific interpretations of human difference, with a host of political repercussions.

Finally, Chapter 5 looks at racism in the context of contemporary immigration and the war on terror. The nexus of asylum seekers, illegal immigrants, terrorists, and Muslims is shown to blend into a single target seen as threatening the West. Draconian immigration controls, racial profiling in anti-terrorist policing, and the roll-back of civil liberties are some of the outcomes of the racialization of the war between the rich and poor worlds under the guise of a so-called "clash of civilizations."

★ ★ ★

In January 2007, the British media was caught in a storm over allegations of racism in the *Celebrity Big Brother* house. The popular reality television program was marred by the racist language used against Indian Hindi movie star, Shilpa Shetty, by a cohort of her housemates. The affair caused a furor with tens of thousands of people calling the British broadcasting regulator to launch their complaint. Ordinary people around the world were outraged about the name-calling and racist stereotyping meted out to the actress. The echo was heard by Britain's top politicians. Tony Blair said that everyone "must oppose racism in all its forms." His successor, Gordon Brown, called for Britain to be "seen as a country of fairness and tolerance" despite the evidence to the contrary from the *Big Brother* house.

Public and vindictive racism of the type exhibited on *Big Brother* disrupts the notion that most Western countries have of themselves as havens of diversity and tolerance. However, much less is said about the everyday banal racism experienced by those whom the sociologist Zygmunt Bauman has referred to as "wasted life" – the illegal immigrants and asylum seekers desperate to seek out a better life, whose bodies are regularly washed up on the shores of Europe's beaches, and the Muslim families whose lives are wrecked by anti-terrorist raids that ultimately reveal nothing. The complex of reasons that causes migration and terrorism, used by Western governments to justify "legal racism," may go unnoticed by many of the same TV viewers who called up in Shilpa's defense. Why this is the case and what it is about the way in which Western societies have evolved that has caused racism to become such a fundamental – yet unspoken and often unseen – element of our lives is the subject of this book. It is a platform for further exploration and, hopefully, debate about how racism can be given the attention it unfortunately still continues to require.

1

Racism, history and politics

Fundamentally, all racism/s are a cultural manifestation, a reflection or expression of tensions or problems within a society, rather than a phenomenon derived from an autonomous and somehow "objective" sphere of scientific investigation and theory.

(MacMaster 2001: 7)

Racism is a political phenomenon rather than a mere set of ideas. To analyze racism we must go beyond the texts of the racial "scientists" and philosophers. Instead we must look at how certain political conditions during particular historical contexts led to some of the ideas proposed by racial theorists being integrated into the political practices of nation-states. This chapter focuses on racism as both a political idea and a practice with effects on policy. Racism is taken to be a modern phenomenon and inherently a Western one. These three aspects – the political nature of racism, its modernity, and its grounding in the history of the West – are fundamental to understanding racism's continuing hold over contemporary Western societies.

Revealing the political foundations of racism is particularly important today. The end of the era of decolonization, of Jim Crow and of apartheid in South Africa, and the establishment of immigration societies across most of the West have led to the shattering of many of the taboos that surrounded racism. Cultural relativism, once an anti-racist tool of the well-meaning left wing, has been turned on its head. Cultural relativists aimed to show that non-European peoples were equal but different to Europeans and that their supposed lack of progress was merely due to the historical "chance," as the anthropologist Claude Lévi-Strauss (1975) put it, that the industrial revolution took place in the West. Today, non-Europeans are portrayed as being equally able to exert force as Europeans. Indeed, they are commonly envisioned as posing a greater threat because, while they have the capacity to damage the West, they are said not to have the level of civility to evaluate the consequences of their actions.

It is common to suggest, therefore, that talk about racism has become redundant. The idea that society is "beyond racism" has important bearings on the way history is told and taught. For example, it has become acceptable to discuss the history of colonialism in a positive light in a way that would not have been possible in recent times. What does this mean for the way in which racism and the various forms it has taken — colonialism, slavery, genocide, and discrimination — are interpreted, taught, and publicly debated?

The popularity of revisionist readings of the history of colonialism and slavery, for example, is not unrelated to the tendency to brush racism under the carpet. For example, historians such as the Harvard Professor Niall Ferguson, whose television series, *Empire: How Britain Made the Modern World*, which presents an historically revisionist account of the positive effects the British Empire had on the lands it colonized, have become bestsellers. The Prime Minister of India, Manmohan Singh, in his address on receiving an honorary doctorate from Oxford University in July 2005, encapsulates this positive reassessment of colonial history:

> Today, with the balance and perspective offered by the passage of time and the benefit of hindsight, it is possible for an Indian Prime Minister to assert that India's experience with Britain had its beneficial consequences too. Our notions of the rule of law, of a Constitutional government, of a free press, of a professional civil service, of modern universities and research laboratories have all been fashioned in the crucible where an age old civilization met the dominant Empire of the day.

The growing acceptability of the revisionist approach to colonial history and its influence on policy making, particularly in education, makes it all the more important to insist on an historicized, political approach to the analysis of racism. When the analysis of racism as an individual attitude, rather than a political idea, is coupled with the drive to frame colonialism in a positive light and blame the problems encountered in diverse societies on the cultural incompatibility of immigrants and their "unhelpful" victimization on the grounds of racism, it becomes even more pressing to analyze racism from a political point of view.

Racism and modernity

In *Race: The History of an Idea in the West*, Ivan Hannaford examines race and racism from antiquity to the twentieth century. He takes a firm stance against the idea that race (namely, fixed biological differences between human groups) has any serious bearing in philosophical, scientific, historical, or philological terms. He calls for us "*not* to accept that the history of Western thought has always been, and will always be, a history of racial thought" (1996: 4). By going so far back in his analysis, Hannaford lends weight to the thesis being put forward here that race really only comes into political being with the advent of modernity.

Hannaford bases his book on three further arguments:

1. The word race as used in Western languages is first found as late as the period 1200–1500. Only in the seventeenth century did it take on a separate meaning from the Latin word *gens*, or clan, and was related to the concept "ethnic group." "In other words," Hannaford insists, "the dispositions and presuppositions of race and ethnicity were introduced – some would say 'invented' or 'fabricated'– in modern times . . ." (ibid. 6) and, in any case, were not given the meaning they have today until after the French and American revolutions.

2. The reason why the notion of race became such a powerful and attractive idea is due to the "deliberate manipulation" of texts by scientists and historians to show that a racial order has always structured humanity. This manipulation is part of the classical tendency to see political processes as the main means of understanding society and the introduction instead of biologized or naturalized accounts of human relations.

3. The idea of race is not proper to Western civilization from a longitudinal historical perspective. Rather it emerges with the Enlightenment as a means of explaining the complexities of modes of human organization such as castes or tribes. However, in Hannaford's view, this explanation is built on a history that has nothing whatsoever to do with race. In other words, race cannot explain the historical evolution of ethnic groups, tribes, or castes.

Hannaford insists that race is both modern and inextricable from politics. There is significant argument about when to date the period known as modernity. For some scholars it is the post-medieval period, from the 1400s and the invention of the printing press; for others it is as late as the period following 1860. I have taken modernity to date back to the Age of Enlightenment, thus, broadly, the eighteenth century: a period of great political transformation made possible by the French revolution, the origins of nation-states as we know them today, and the beginnings of technological and scientific "advancement." How does identifying the emergence of racism with the development of Enlightenment thought help us to understand the modernity of racism?

Hannaford divides the period over which the idea of race develops into three stages: 1684–1815, 1815–1870, and 1870–1914. This final period is known as the "Golden Age" of racism, a time when it was possible for the British Prime Minister of the time, Benjamin Disraeli, to proclaim: "Race is all. There is no other truth."

The word "race" is first used in its modern sense in 1684 when François Bernier published his *"Nouvelle division de la terre par les différents espèces ou races qui l'habitent."* In Bernier's essay, race stands for divisions among humans based on observable physical differences. At this stage, race is used as a simple descriptor and there is no intention of superiority or inferiority meant by presenting humanity in this way. Nonetheless, dividing humanity up in the manner proposed by Bernier would have been impossible only years earlier. Radical changes in methodology at this time made it possible to speak about humanity being divided into proposed "races." It is this methodological shift in the way Western scholars started to think about what it means to be human that fundamentally changed the way we think about the origins of human life, the universe, and society. It is the basis for the way we think about these things to this day.

The most significant change was in the fact that theological and metaphysical explanations about life and the universe were replaced by a "more logical description and classifications that ordered humankind in terms of physiological and mental criteria based on observable 'facts' and tested evidence" (Hannaford, 1996: 187). Philosophers like René Descartes, Thomas Hobbes, and John Locke, who are largely synonymous with the evolution of Enlightenment thought, along with others such as Immanuel Kant, were responsible for these important changes. The rational thought, based on observable evidence, that these thinkers initiated made it possible for things to be divided and classified systematically. This ordering procedure could be applied to everything, living or not, but where it took on the greatest importance was in reference to humans.

Based on the newly discovered possibility of thinking about the development of humanity in rational terms, several scholars – most influentially Johann Friedrich Blumenbach (1752–1840) – began to question the classical (Aristotelian) political tradition. Politics at the time of the Enlightenment challenged the absolute sovereignty of a monarch over his or her people. The French revolution eventually proved that kings did not have a divine right to rule. These challenges led to questions about where the legitimacy for rule *did* come from. Several scholars, using new methods of classification that saw human beings within a general scheme of things that included all species, posited the natural origins of contemporary politics as an alternative to the Greco-Roman roots subscribed to by Europeans until this stage. The growing influence of the study of natural history by the mid-eighteenth century, while as yet unable to refute completely either the Bible or the classical tradition, sowed the seeds for alternative accounts of the origins of humankind (e.g. evolution), no longer traced uniquely back to Jerusalem, Greece, and Rome.

MacMaster has made it clear that, at the time of Enlightenment, racial divisions cannot be seen as having the same pernicious connotations associated with the racism of later years. Nevertheless, it is important to look back to this time in order to understand the influence of Enlightenment thought on the evolution of full-scale modern racism.

The rational ordering and classification of people into biologically determined groups made possible by advances in thought at this time, and the nascent challenges to traditional interpretations of the origins of humankind based on classical and biblical accounts were fundamental to the eruption of racism by the late eighteenth century. However, racism – an inherently political phenomenon – could not take root in the absence of favorable political conditions that the rise of nationalism and anti-Enlightenment thinking brought about.

MacMaster shows that ideas about racial differences between human groups that were developed during the Age of Enlightenment actually upheld the thesis of monogenesis: the idea that all human beings are descended from one original group. What he calls "humanitarian racism" can be distinguished from the racism that emerges following 1870, in that it remains faithful both to the biblical notion of Creation and to Enlightenment ideals of the brotherhood of man. At this time, physical anthropologists, such as Blumenbach, who based their work on the accounts of "travel writers" (missionaries, soldiers, or so-called explorers), saw all races as the descendents of one ancestral group. This group was believed to be white-skinned. Non-white races were understood to have "degenerated" over time due to climate, disease, and way of life.

Around the time of the 1789 French revolution, Enlightenment principles of equality encouraged the gradual abolition of slavery and the emancipation of European Jewry by the mid-nineteenth century. This movement was seen as being entirely compatible with developments in the classification of races. The task of the European or white race, as direct descendents of the ancestors of all races, and, as it was believed, the natural rulers over the earth, was to ensure the spread of human progress. The "civilizing mission" was seen as being the responsibility of the Europeans towards the "primitive peoples." Although the racism of the Enlightenment has been seen as less harmful than the exclusionary and violent racism that followed it, its effects, particularly in the colonies, were just as damaging. It is in fact the seemingly paradoxical meeting of Enlightenment principles of humanism with reactionary nationalism that creates the conditions for racism to develop both in Europe and in the colonized world.

No science without politics

The German philosopher Eric Voegelin wrote two volumes on race that he published in 1933 after fleeing Nazi Germany. Voegelin was interested in race as being one of the main ideas structuring a theory of state. He believed that understanding race helps us to understand the nature of the state and politics. Voegelin wrote at a time when racism in Europe was coming to full political fruition with the rise of the Nazis to power. Since Voegelin, few authors have seen race as so fundamental to an understanding of politics, a fact that has led to racism being treated as marginal to state processes. What Voegelin helps us to understand is that racial science would be of no concern were it not for its influence on the political realm in Europe over the eighteenth and nineteenth centuries.

Voegelin distinguishes between the concept and the idea of race. He sees the scientific concept of race as composed of a set of false notions with no actual basis in provable scientific fact. It is the race idea – a well-ordered system of political dogmas – that interests him. Voegelin's approach demonstrates the importance of seeing the development of racial science from a political point of view. The pseudo-scientific notions that are now understood to be at the basis of racism could only have become as important as they did because they found resonance with political movements and agendas. Before turning to these agendas, in particular the ever closer relationship between racism and nationalism by the mid-nineteenth century, let us take a closer look at the main developments in the "race concept" from the Enlightenment to the Romantic period.

Hanniaford (1996: 214) points out that race only came into its own when it "developed a *will* to individual power based on a biology that distinguished superior and inferior races." As we have seen, this was not the intention of the physical anthropologists of the Enlightenment such as Montesquieu or Blumenbach whose interest remained focused on thinking about humanity in terms of the laws of nature more generally. What steps had to be taken to move from a belief in monogenesis to one in polygenesis: the idea that different groups descended from various ancestral groups, an idea that radically diverges from the belief in Creation and the basic brotherhood of man?

The first step was that of racial determinism. The British anatomist Robert Knox, in his *The Races of Men* (1850), set out the notion of an absolute biological divide between races. Knox believed that the impermeability of each racial group made it impossible for races to mix. He saw all racial groups as unchanging over time, as was the hierarchical structure in which they were placed: the white European at the top, the "negro" at the bottom. The former was therefore destined to dominate the latter. MacMaster argues that the development of both racial determinism and polygenesis, as guiding concepts in the formulation of race theory, led to the emergence of rac*ism*. The idea that different human groups did not share the same ancestral lineage and were historically distinct from each other made it easier to believe in the destiny of white people to dominate "inferior" races. We can see how the development of racial science in this direction facilitates the marriage between science and politics: a belief in the inferiority of blacks legitimated their domination and extermination as a consequence of the expanding imperialist politics of the time.

These developments in racial science also led theorists to distinguish among European peoples, and not only between Europeans as a group – once seen as belonging to a single racial block – and non-European others. This racial subdivision of Europeans is central. It explains how race and nation come to be seen as synonymous and, therefore, how imperial competition and war between the European powers could be framed in racial terms. This "self-referential" racism also explains how, in the period between 1870 and 1914, preserving the strong race from degeneration became a primary political concern.

A growing number of scholars became interested in the theme of race. Key figures of the European philosophical corpus, including Immanuel Kant, David Hume, Edmund Burke, and Johann Gottfried Herder, wrote on race in different ways. But these thinkers cannot be called racial scientists. Self-proclaimed racial scientists such as Arthur de Gobineau, Francis Galton, or Georges Vacher de Lapouge, active towards the end of the nineteenth century, were rather more populist than the former group and were directly interested in influencing politics with their ideas. Racism endures politically because it borrows from a variety of discourses and justifications, chopping and changing between them according to context and time.

In order to demonstrate the growth of the union between racial science and the political sphere, the work of two theorists in particular should be considered. In quite different ways, the work of Count Arthur de Gobineau and Charles Darwin has become synonymous with the history of racial science of the nineteenth century. The work of these two personalities is explanatory because their contributions had a direct influence on the marriage between politics and racial science. For Gobineau, this was determined by his mission to alter the course of politics radically and steer the European states away from the dangers he associated with the greater equality brought about by Enlightenment. Darwin's work is crucial mainly because of the way it was interpreted by the Social Darwinists as a system for justifying social engineering: eugenics.

Count Arthur de Gobineau (1816–1882) was a French aristocrat whose contribution to racial science was based on his preoccupation with what he saw as the *degeneration* of Europe. He had an important influence on German racism at the turn of the twentieth century be-cause of what his theory revealed about Europeans themselves: faced with unleashed hordes of emancipated Jews and working classes, the white race was in danger of deterioration from within. The basis of his theory of race was that no other factor – climate, geography, and so on – had any impact on the place of a nation in the echelon of civilization. And one race alone was at the origin of "everything great, noble and fruitful in the works of man on this earth" (1915: xv): the white race. These achievements belong "to one family alone, the different branches of which have reigned in all the civilized countries of the universe."

In 1854, Gobineau published his *Essai sur l'inégalité des races humaines*. However, it was only ten years later, following the American Civil War and the Franco-Prussian War, that his ideas had any great influence. He sought to use race to explain the ills of the age, particularly the threat to aristocratic rule from working-class consciousness, the corruption of the Church, and what he saw as the spread of Semitic values. He blamed these ills on the degeneration of the European people. This had come about due to a "bastardization" of European civilization whose people's blood was no longer pure, having mixed for too long with other infe-rior races.

The only way to redeem the race was to ensure that no blood was mixed and that purity was upheld. This was vital because, for Gobineau, only the character of a people determined the place of a nation on the scale of progress. No other factor, be it historical or geographical, could have any influence over what nations could achieve: race was all. His position, reflected in the title of his essay, was that there could be no equality between races. He rejected the efforts made by some in the United States of America to elevate the status of blacks and Native Americans. He saw slavery as emblematic of the natural inferiority of non-Europeans. Any attempt towards equality would disturb the natural order of things.

Two factors in his stance are important for understanding how racism developed on the political stage during the mid-nineteenth century, reaching beyond the realms of mere scholarly interest. First, Gobineau's belief in the primacy of race meant a rejection of politics. No political processes could change the course of a civilization. Its place was determined by ancestry and blood alone. The nation was comparable to the human body. Culture played no part in determining a people's fate; only a well-functioning "anatomy" could ensure its progress. This meant that politics in the traditional Greco-Roman sense became reduced to nature, blood, and the race war. The growing influence of this way of thinking on nationalist ideologues is vital for understanding how racism later became so central to the policies of states, as it was for the colonial administrations, the southern states of the US, and the Nazism and fascism of the twentieth century.

Second, his stance on race was a direct reaction against Enlightenment principles of humanism. The growth of Romanticism and nationalism in the mid-nineteenth century represented a conservative reaction against the emancipatory nature of Enlightenment ideals. In practical terms, Gobineau's racism was motivated by the fear of the aristocratic class's loss of power. The working class in Europe was beginning to emerge as a real contender for political power. The gradual extension of the right to vote to all men and the spread of Marxist thinking were crucial factors. The aristocracy had reason to fear this movement. Gobineau's contribution was to explain the right of the ruling classes to rule in natural terms. Therefore, not only did his brand of racism condemn blacks to eternal slavery, it also divided the social classes in Europe into racial categories. It was this thinking that paved the way for eugenics to emerge later as a "solution" to Europe's social ills.

The work of Charles Darwin on the origin of species (1859) radically transformed our understanding of the evolution of life-forms. Darwin himself, a practicing Christian, was concerned with not openly challenging Christian doctrine. He therefore did not extend his theory of natural selection to humans. However, his work had subversive possibilities at a time when racial theorists were looking for more systematic ways to frame their ideas, and it was, inevitably, put to the service of the race idea.

The great addition made by Darwin's theory was that it was able to provide a mechanical explanation of natural processes that race scientists such as Gobineau claimed governed human life and society. The theory of evolution with its explanation of each slow step of development was the missing part in the puzzle. When added to the work on race, Darwin's ideas on evolution, natural selection, and the survival of the fittest made it possible for the idea of evolving, self-determining races to come about. Notions about the natural superiority of one race and its destiny to rule over others could previously have been refuted on the grounds that they could not explain how races actually emerged. When married to Darwinian theory, the ideas of Gobineau and others on the inequality of races could be shown to have a basis in natural history, the result of a long and painfully slow evolutionary battle for supremacy between naturally emerging human groups.

Darwin's theory of evolution and its social interpretations had two main consequences for politics. First, his work represents the final stage in the naturalization of society and politics: the final break with the classical tradition that saw shared interests leading to individual thought and action as the main determinants of politics. Instead, political and social life were equated with natural existence. Everything could now be related to biological cycles and genetic functioning. As Hannaford (1996: 273) puts it, after Darwin, the belief was that "the condition of human society depended for explanation more on the principles of natural selection and evolution than upon the quality of political institutions." The mechanism that Darwin's theory offered for explaining the apparent naturalness of these processes gave credence to racial scientists' convictions about the biologically preordained right of the white race to rule over all others.

The second important influence was the interpretation of natural selection made by Social Darwinists. These followers of Darwin believed that natural selection ensured that the stronger of the species survived, leaving the weaker, unable to adapt to the environment, to die out. It was through Social Darwinists like Karl Pearson that the *Origin of Species* had the greatest political influence, contributing to the rise of racism's importance as a core idea that was to structure Western politics in the period after 1870. The formulation of Darwinian thought in racial terms led to the belief that, in order to ensure the survival of the human species, it was necessary for stronger and superior race nations to vanquish their weaker competitors. Life was based on a constant struggle to maintain superiority that was seen as beneficial to humanity as a whole: there was simply no room for "degeneracy" and resultant weakening of the race.

Social Darwinism's main political influence was domestic. It gave credence to a class racism promoted by a bourgeoisie faced with the growth of poverty in the proletarian urban slums. The Social Darwinism of an academic such as Ernst Haeckel at the turn of the twentieth century is a not untypical example of Darwin's theories pushed to their social limits. Haeckel's monist philosophy was based on the idea that the strongest of race nations had a duty to dominate over others in the interests of the whole of humankind. According to the logic of the "survival of the fittest," the loss of individual human lives was justifiable in the interest of preserving the race. In social terms, this meant that weak individuals, such as the sick or disabled, could be exterminated according to the principles of eugenic purification.

These ideas became increasingly popular after 1860, and in particular after Francis Galton's coining, in 1883, of the term "eugenics." Positive eugenics – the strengthening of the race through planned breeding – and negative eugenics – the inhibition of the development of the "racially feeble" – were both widely debated. Eugenic ideas were often linked to discussions about the virtues of social welfare. The poor were seen as racially degenerate, rife with disease, alcoholism, and mental instability. Social welfare programs were understood by the most extreme proponents of negative eugenics as keeping alive a class whose disappearance would only serve to strengthen the race overall.

As MacMaster takes care to point out, the eugenics movement rarely had a direct influence on policy making in Europe before Nazism in Germany. Nevertheless, the popularity of eugenicist ideas meant that they entered into common consciousness. Eugenicists caused the average individual to believe in the possibility of human engineering and introduced notions such as "half-caste" into popular language, spreading the idea that the so-called inferior races bred like animals and must, like them, be controlled. Moreover, it attracted many of the foremost thinkers of the late nineteenth and early twentieth centuries. These included Margaret Sanger, the instigator of family planning in the USA, and Beatrice and Sydney Webb, founders of the Socialist Fabian Society in Britain. Winston Churchill was a vice president of the First International Eugenics Congress held in 1912. His belief in eugenicist ideas of sterilization led to the passing of the Mental Deficiency Act in the UK in 1913, although it did not lead to any sterilizations being carried out.

Race and state: towards the race nation

In practice, how did the ideas of racial scientists infuse politics to the extent that they did over the course of the nineteenth and twentieth centuries? What was the connection between the rise of nationalism and racism? And what is meant by the concept of race nation?

Although it is difficult to think about a time before nations, there is considerable evidence that they are an intrinsically modern phenomenon. So, despite the fact that living together as part of a national group within a specific territory appears to many people to be the only logical or viable way of organizing society, this was not always the case. Indeed, historians such as Eric Hobsbawm propose that it is the ideology of nationalism that convinces us that nations are ancient. According to Hobsbawm, nationalist political movements *invented* nations and the necessary myths, symbols, rituals, ceremonies, and historical figures that they require to constitute and reconstitute themselves. In a similar vein, the sociologist Ernest Gellner argued that nations "do not have a navel." In other words, there is no way of tracing a people's lineage back to pre-modern times, as proponents of the ethno-symbolist approach to the study of nations and nationalism, such as Anthony Smith, would have it. On the contrary, the nation emerges in response to the requirements of an industrial-capitalist society. Elites used the concept of nation to make sense of the complexity brought about by industrialization and capitalism.

While the origins of nations have been hotly debated, there is general agreement that nationalism and the nation-state emerged out of the nineteenth-century Romantic movement. The fathers of nationalism, such as the Germans Herder and Fichte, mounted a conservative reaction to the universalist and rationalist cosmopolitanism of the Enlightenment. Instead they called for the state to be driven by the common purpose of a people sharing a common ancestry, and thus a single destiny. In sum, nations do not predate nationalism. It is nationalism that breeds nations and brings about the union of nation and state.

Following the rise of the Romanticists during the mid-nineteenth century, the ideas of race and nation came to be used synonymously within politics. Ludwig Gumplowicz (1838–1909) was an influential race thinker and sociologist who first made the link between race and state in his book, *Rasse und Staat*, published in 1875. As Hannaford points out, in Gumplowicz's thought, the state is subsumed under the nation that is linked inextricably to race. For Gumplowicz, the Aristotelian theory of state that was commonly seen to underpin modern state theory was irrelevant. A state was nothing more than the people who lived within it. It could grow if it was successful in conquest and depending on the laws of nature, which could only be discovered by analyzing ethnic and social groups. It was these, rather than the individual so highly regarded by Enlightenment thought, which were important for understanding nation-states. The individual counted for nothing. The notion of the "Natural Rights of Man" or "Reason" were, therefore, laughable in Gumplowicz's eyes. The individual was completely subsumed under the state which was governed by the rules of nature or racial law. Consequently, the only option is race war because it is only through competition with other races (nations) that the state can act. His thinking was of paramount importance for the development of twentieth-century race relations theory. He subsumed everything – "moral, juridical, economic, and aesthetic advances" (Hannaford 1996: 302) – under the conflict between races. Political success on an international level was now based both on the possibility of unifying the "race nation" internally and competing with and dominating other race nations abroad.

The context for this analysis of political life was both domestic and international. Within the European states where racist theory and politics intertwined, the context was nation-building. On the international front, it was imperialism and colonialism that were all-important for an understanding of race's growth in political status. As Philip Yale Nicholson (1999: 7) makes clear, these two contexts are interdependent:

> People were turned into races when nations extended and defined their political hegemony through conquest and expropriation. Race and nation were born and raised together; they are the Siamese twins of modernity.

Racism, as we know it today, has its origins in the need for Europeans to define themselves internally as nations. Made possible by the Enlightenment obsession with ordering and classification, race provides the reason for the differences between human beings. In an age of rampant expansionism characteristic of nineteenth-century imperialism, race also functions to differentiate between Europeans and non-Europeans. Indeed, Europe is identified through the comparison with everything that it is perceived *not* to be. Race functions in the service of nationalism and the nation-building process because it provides the scientific proof for why members of a nation are meant to share a common destiny. And what better proof than the comparison of progressive, aesthetic, and cultured Europe with primitive, dark, and chaotic "non-Europe"?

The consolidation of the race nation, defined in relation to inferior outsiders, was not immediate. It proceeded in two stages. The first was focused internally, the second externally. In other words, in Europe, racism targeted its own populations before setting its sights on outsiders. At this stage, the colonies were thought of as completely separate from Europe. Although images of dark and dangerous "natives" fed the popular imagination, they were in fact related to European insiders, mainly in the first instance the working class and Jews. It is this focus on the internal racial degradation of society that gave rise to the state's policies of surveillance and control (biopolitics) that, from their outset, were racial in the sense that they sought to classify groups, weeding out the racially valuable from the racially worthless. The growth in state power in this domain, often using techniques already used in the colonies, was later applied to the separation of citizens from "aliens" that was to become definitive of the modern racism of the state.

As we have seen, the popularity of Social Darwinist ideas and the development of eugenics were important factors that contributed to the politicization of racism in late nineteenth-century Europe. The working classes were a favored target of eugenicists. Jews, blacks, and the working class were seen as "feeble minded." The intimation of the eugenicists was that, if the survival of the race was to be ensured, feeble-mindedness in the population had to be curtailed.

More generally, the widespread idea of *self-referential racism*, that saw the nation as a race whose strength needed to be protected, instilled a belief among elites that the working class was degenerate: it would be responsible for the collapse of the race as a whole. As Balibar notes (1991: 209), "criminality, congenital vice (alcohol and drugs), physical and moral defects, dirtiness, sexual diseases" were painted as being pathological among these classes. The idea that the working class posed a threat to the nation at this time had emphatically political roots. Racialization functioned to demonize and scapegoat "dangerous" political groups, pathologizing what is in fact a political rather than an inherent threat based on supposed "degeneracy."

This political threat was rising class-consciousness. In the late nineteenth and early twentieth centuries, workers in both the USA and

Europe were becoming increasingly attracted to the idea of an international proletariat, and were joining together to struggle for their rights. The working classes were seen by elites as capable of morally subverting the nation. The potential in their strength, and the crucial fact that workers identified with each other across borders, could be a death blow to the idea of the unified race nation. Michel Foucault saw "race war" as a direct competitor of "class war." For Foucault, the threat of class war was perceived by elites to be so strong that the conflicting notion of race war is brought in to quell it. Something had to be done to ensure that the people would not be swayed by the appeal of internationalism. The idea of the unified race nation and the uniqueness of its inhabitants – the people, all contributing to its success and strength – was used to sway them. The degeneracy of the working class, but also of the Jews, portrayed both as the fomenters of communist revolution and as the robbers of international capitalism, was used to pit classes and ethnicities against each other in a struggle for the ownership of national destiny.

W.E.B. Du Bois, the African-American scholar of race relations, famously predicted that the problem of the twentieth century would be that of the "color line." For Du Bois, the internal stratification of US and European societies along class and ethnic/religious lines, interpreted as racial divides, mirrored the situation in the colonized lands. The hierarchical relationship between colonizer and colonized that dehumanized the latter predated and influenced racialization *within* Western societies. Crucially, as Balibar points out, the stratification of whites into classes or races lost its significance in the colonial situation. Any white man in the colonies could reinvent himself as belonging to a higher class and treated those he colonized as inferior to himself regardless of his own status at home. As Du Bois (1946: 312) poignantly reminds us, the oppression of the working class in Europe did little to change the fact that "the white people of Europe had a right to live upon the labor and property of the colored peoples of the world."

In Europe, partly due to the growing importance of the competition for imperial domination, the focus gradually turned away from racial degradation to *racial unity*. There were two main motivations for this. First, the racialization of the working class did nothing to rally them to the cause of growing industrialization. Much like today, when the majority of big business opposes strict immigration controls, the proposals of the nineteenth-century eugenicists had little influence on capitalists or the political leaders who supported them. Quite simply, if European nations were to compete economically, the poor were needed for work. Second, what MacMaster calls the "racialization of European nationalism" was mainly achieved between the Franco-Prussian War (1870–1871) and the First World War (1914–1918). Mass numbers were needed to fight these wars. Moreover, a sense of belonging to the nation had to be instilled if the masses were to be prepared to die for it. While previously, eugenicists had suggested that charity was wasted on the poor whose continued existence would reduce the strength of the race, now social welfare was introduced as a means of improving the nation's efficiency. This served the dual purpose of quelling revolutionary impulses among the disenfranchised poor and working classes and including them in the project of national "greatness." Needless to say, none of this did anything actually to empower the poor, but it did have the intended consequence of quelling internationalism, with trade unionism becoming more and more national in focus.

The unifying of race and nation and the more general cementing of the nationalist political project led to a dividing line being drawn between insiders and outsiders. Competition with other nations for imperialist, economic, and territorial domination at this time strengthened nations internally and pitted them against each other. It was in this spirit that control over foreigners living within the national territory began and the first immigration controls were introduced.

Today, it is difficult to imagine a time when people of all nationalities were free to move and settle in other countries without the restrictions of immigration law. Yet, despite the fact that foreign populations were certainly constrained in various ways under the rule of foreign kings, it was not before the full consolidation of the nation-state that the right to enter and stay in a country became a legal matter. Laws excluding certain groups of people from immigrating were not introduced before the end of the nineteenth century either in the USA or Europe.

Michel Foucault relates his theory of bio-power to the introduction of immigration controls at this time. During the 1880s, Western nation-states were moving away from liberal principles of *laissez-faire* towards more protectionist policies (Noiriel 1991). States were taking greater responsibility for the welfare of their populations, but this also meant that they were more active in their quantification and surveillance. The science of demography was born at this time as a so-called "science of the state." With it came the idea that governments should have concrete knowledge of who lived on the national territory. This had the dual purpose of protection and control and cannot be separated from ideas about race. As the synonymy of race and nation reached its peak, demography reflected the primacy of race thinking at the time. In an age when each race nation was seen to exist within a competitive international system, the question of who could be an insider was all-important.

Immigration laws in the US were first introduced in 1882 to restrict the entry of Chinese laborers. The act was amended in 1884 to be applied to all ethnic Chinese regardless of their country of origin. But as early as 1862, the state of California passed the Anti-Coolie Act to "protect free white labor from competition from Chinese Coolie labor and to discourage the immigration of the Chinese into the State of California." In France, the first immigration laws were introduced in 1889, while in Britain, the Aliens' Act was first passed in 1905. As the US example shows clearly, this new type of legislation was based on the increasingly accepted view that residents of a country could be divided into insiders and outsiders. The former belonged, racially and culturally, to the nation. The latter could, under certain conditions, be granted the right to enjoy the benefits of citizenship but would never be conceived of as full members of the race nation.

This binary conceptualization of the "social body" also began to affect groups who had lived within the national territory for a longer period of time. Just where the line was to be drawn between insider and outsider was increasingly determined by notions about race based on skin color, ethnic origin, and religion. The racialization of the state is embodied by the drawing of this line. From now on, state policy could be based on a vision of the nation that was based on racial classification. To this day, immigration into Western states is determined by principles that are based on racial conceptions of insiders and outsiders. Despite the official denial of racial categories, they continue to shape policies and attitudes to non-white settlement.

Two types of racism: naturalism and historicism

We are beginning to see how ideas about race had influence in many spheres by the late nineteenth century. Racism, therefore, can never be reduced to one concrete phenomenon that is easy to pin down. That is why several scholars in recent years have preferred to talk about racisms in the plural.

David Goldberg lays the foundations for understanding racism's multiplicity. In *The Racial State* he argues that "there are generalizable conditions in virtue of which the modern state is to be conceived as racial, and as racially exclusionary, or racist" (2002: 2), an argument we shall return to in the course of this book. In constructing his analysis, he iterates two types of racism that continue to coexist and define the nature of racism from the dawn of the modern era to the present day. These two forms, although apparently incompatible, are the key for conceiving of how racism continues to function despite the prevalently held idea that it has been in decline since the mid-twentieth century. Understanding how they operate will in turn help us to understand how racism is experienced, not only as the direct injustice of slavery, lynching, and genocide, but also as the humdrum of racial stereotyping, criminalization, and discrimination.

Goldberg argues that all modern nation-states are racial, but that not all states are actively *racist* in the formal sense, as in the case of apartheid South Africa, for example. He identifies two logics that he claims define the various forms of "racial rule": racial *naturalism* and racial *historicism*. When do they originate?

> The naturalist conception, the claim of inherent racial inferiority, dominated from the seventeenth well into the nineteenth-century; the historicist or progressivist commitment concerning itself with contrasting claims of historical immaturity displaced the dominance of naturalism in the second half of the nineteenth-century but far from eclipsed it. (2002: 74)

The two logics, therefore, overlap historically and, as will become clear, they continued to do so well into our times. To understand the great significance of race politically, Goldberg argues, it is vital to look at its alliance with the modern state. As we saw in the previous chapter, racism cannot thrive without politics and its political home is the modern Western nation-state. The two forms of racism, both naturalist and historicist, are based on their variable abilities, in different times and contexts and sometimes at once, to benefit the politics of running these highly complex political machines called states. Goldberg traces the origins of these different types of racial rule back to the competing approaches to modern state politics of European philosophers. His argument is that race served a significant purpose within their conceptualizations of the state and human relations in early modern times. The main reference for the ideas constructed around race was the "native" found living in the lands newly "discovered" by European explorers; lands and peoples soon to be appropriated by their Western "discoverers."

Naturalist racism is the idea that the negative characteristics associated with these dark-skinned natives, so different to the white-skinned ideal of humanity created by Europeans in their own image, are immutable. In other words, the native is seen as incapable of changing. She is and will always remain a primitive being, a creature without history, incapable of progress. Europeans conceived of themselves as evolved human beings who had progressed over countless centuries to acquire the knowledge and culture that enabled them to dominate the globe. Their dark-skinned counterparts, in contrast, were condemned to eternal primitiveness. If having a history is the mark of a progressive society, one that can trace its roots and track its evolution, "native society" was timeless, "simply 'there,' fixed in time" (Goldberg 2002: 43).

This sharp contrast drawn between the "civilized" and the "natives" is also emphasized by Stuart Hall, who refers to racialized discourse as based on a series of "binary oppositions." On the one hand, Europeans refer to themselves in terms that evoke culture – "refinement, learning and knowledge, a belief in reason, the presence of developed institutions ..." (1997a: 243) – while the "black races" are referred to in naturalized or instinctual terms:

> the open expression of emotion and feeling rather than intellect, a lack of "civilized refinement" in sexual and social life, a reliance on custom and ritual, and lack of developed civil institutions.

Goldberg recalls the importance of Thomas Hobbes's (1588–1679) theorization of the modern state for our understanding of racial naturalism. Hobbes saw the modern state as a necessary means of saving society from the permanent insecurity of what he called the "State of Nature." If the modern state was to succeed, it would have to be portrayed as permanent and solid. It stood in contrast to the chaos represented by statelessness. In the context of the "discoveries," the territories inhabited by racial others were representative of statelessness. The fathers of European philosophy all referred to the lives of "natives," "savages," "Indians," or "Negroes"to exemplify their conceptions of the State of Nature. To warn against a failure to accept the state, philosophers from Hobbes to Rousseau pointed to these examples of strange, apparently incomplete, humanity where only chaos and anarchy reigned.

However, there is no idea in Hobbes, for example, that the American "Indians" he described could one day attain a higher state of being and escape the State of Nature. Contradicting his own theory that Europeans once lived in the State of Nature from which the modern state offered them the way out, he sees the native as forever trapped within it. For him, the "discovered" lands were found in their "pristine state, occupied if at all by those in their 'natural,'"undeveloped condition"(Goldberg 2002: 42). The idea is clearly that whereas the "civilized"peoples have the inherent wherewithal to go beyond the State of Nature, this would be impossible for the "primitive." Hobbes's logic fixes "racially conceived 'Natives' in a prehistorical condition of pure Being naturally incapable of development and so historical progress" (Goldberg 2002: 43).

We can all recognize this conception of race as the foundation for base, overt racism. Slavery, segregation, and the appalling injustices of apartheid were all based on an idea, promoted and facilitated by the state, that blacks and other religious or ethnic minorities were inferior to whites. Naturalism is at the heart of the white supremacist reading of history in which whites are destined to dominate non-whites. As racial science progressed, "scientific" legitimation was found to justify this idea and give weight to unjust, but highly profitable, systems (slavery, colonialism, apartheid) that necessitated racial rule. Naturalist racism is what we automatically think of when we consider the question, "what is racism?" It was the racism of coercive states such as the southern United States before 1965 and South Africa until 1994. In these types of regime, "the racially dominant were seen to set laws, impose order, and maintain control because destined by blood and genes to do so" (Goldberg 2002: 75).

Being dominant was not seen as a question of chance. It was seen as a people's natural destiny. This racism, based on the purity of blood and the strict separation of racial inferiors from the dominant race, continues to inspire groups on the extreme right. How does this brand of racism, quick to be condemned by the majority of those across the political spectrum today, differ from Goldberg's other racial scheme, historicism or progressivism?

Goldberg's second type of racial thought is known alternatively as historicist or progressivist racism because of its dependence on both history and progress as explanations for white supremacism. For historicists, it was not that the "natives" were inherently savage and thus irredeemable, as the proponents of racial naturalism would have it, but that Europeans dominated "primitive others" because the former were historically developed. Europeans had progressed, while non-Europeans remained in a state of primitiveness. This view does not deny that non-Europeans have the capacity for progress, but argues that it is only under the tutelage of the more advanced White Man that such progress can ever come about. Racial historicism is the ultimate legitimation of colonial domination because it is based not on the base subjugation of the "primitive native" but on her elevation to a better life that only the presence of the colonizer as a guide will ensure.

Goldberg sees the philosopher John Locke (1632–1704) as one of the earliest proponents of this line of reasoning, although he argues that the tension between naturalism and historicism can be traced back to the origins of racial thought. Locke's historicism can be traced through to the writings of the nineteenth-century empiricists, Auguste Comte and J.S. Mill, as well as Karl Marx, who saw colonialism as providing the necessary conditions for socialist revolution. Locke, who himself held stock in the Royal Africa Company and justified slavery, is, according to Goldberg, often misread as a racial naturalist. However, Locke opposed the idea of essentialism, that is of fixing or naturalizing individuals' identities. He therefore did not advocate slavery because of a belief that enslavement was the natural state of "primitives," as Hobbes would have done. In contrast, Locke likened slaves to children who could not be treated as equals. The implication is that, like children, slaves "grow up." Therefore, Locke thought that slaves could attain equality over time.

This line of thought that, as Goldberg points out, is much harder to pin down than the brutishness of naturalism, shaped much of the thinking about the relationship between Europeans and non-Europeans, colonizers and colonized, for the centuries to come. Indeed, it formed the basis for arguments against decolonization well after the official abolition of slavery in the early nineteenth century. Racial historicist attitudes framed debates about the ability of the colonized to rule themselves. It was the basis for fears that, as nations, the colonized were too immature for self-government and that they would fall back into chaos if the Europeans were to retreat. The campaign to end slavery, culminating in the British emancipation of slaves in 1834, was fed by a belief in Europe's "civilizing mission" in "underdeveloped" lands. If progress and inclusion in history were to be achieved, it was not by the whip but through education, guidance, and the establishment of an infrastructure – the colonial administration whose systems continue to form the basis of government in many former colonies – that this would come about.

The explicitness of the belief that it was only through education in Western ways that progress in the colonies could be ensured is illustrated by "Macaulay's Minute on Indian Education." In a speech to Parliament in 1835, Macaulay, a member of the British Supreme Council of India, advocated that schools devoted to the teaching of Sanskrit or Arabic should be closed down because "English is better worth knowing." In what follows, it is clear that, in addition to Macaulay's real belief that Indians would benefit from forgetting their own languages and immersing themselves in English, he sees the creation of an English-speaking class in India as essential for colonial governance:

> We must at present do our best to form a class who may be interpreters between us and the millions whom we govern; a class of persons, Indian in blood and color, but English in taste, in opinions, in morals, and in intellect. To that class we may leave it to refine the vernacular dialects of the country, to enrich those dialects with terms of science borrowed from the Western nomenclature, and to render them by degrees fit vehicles for conveying knowledge to the great mass of the population.

It is clear how such arguments, debated by philosophers and politicians, could be used in the nineteenth and early twentieth centuries as neat legitimations for the continuing expropriation of colonized lands for the benefit of ever-expanding and competitive European states. As Goldberg shows, both the expansionist colonial project and the mission of civilizing the colonized were justified by an appeal to Reason. Racial historicism was rational while naturalism was the preserve of unreason. It is this that makes historicist racism truly modern: it belonged to the scheme that saw the modern nation-state as destined to spread rationality and progress, both at home and abroad. For Goldberg,

> [M]odern states expand their scope of authority, legitimacy, power, wealth, and control not only over their citizens – in the name of freedom, autonomy, self-determination, and self-direction – but also over those racially considered incapable or not yet capable of self-rule. (2002: 50–1)

The question remains whether racial historicism provides for the possibility of "self-rule," or autonomy more generally, to ever be achieved. Indeed, this question provides us with a clue as to why progressivist racism persists to this day. For many migrants and black and minority ethnic people in contemporary societies, full social inclusion is experienced as just out of reach and dependent on achieving a host of ambiguous and seemingly unattainable targets.

This description of the theoretical differences between racial naturalism and historicism is important because it highlights the various rationales that prop up what Goldberg calls "*racial rule*." As he makes clear, naturalism and historicism coexisted until historicism gradually took the upper hand – but did not erase naturalism – by the mid-1800s. The distinction between naturalist and historicist racism should not lead to the conclusion that the latter was necessarily "better" than the former, nor that historicism has completely eclipsed naturalism. In many instances, the existence of an ideologically historicist set of legitimations may have facilitated the continuity of abhorrent racist practices. In specific cases, such as the United States until the abolition of segregation, racism of the naturalist and the progressivist types coexisted in one country. It may simply be that the baldness of naturalist racism became uncomfortable, especially following the end of the Holocaust, and the struggles of anti-colonialists and civil rights activists. This is obvious in today's context when it is unacceptable, and even illegal in many countries, to use deliberately racist language. We decry the blatant hate speech of the extreme right or of Holocaust deniers. However, racial naturalism has not disappeared. Beyond the obvious spaces of the racist extreme right, it remains present in the protected confines of academia, for example, where the disciplines of genetics and psychology, but also of politics, are used as cover for arguments about the inherent mental inferiority of blacks (cf. Herrnstein and Murray 1994) that do not differ substantially from the naturalist argument of Hobbes, Kant, or Rousseau or of the racial scientists themselves.

However, neither should historicism be seen as a cover-up for naturalism, as though this were racism's "real" agenda. Both have a purpose and, as Goldberg points out (2002: 46), racial historicism "can be equal to racial naturalism in its biased presumption, its ignorant projection, and its violent denials of any virtues but its own." Whether by condemning the "native" to a life of savagery, forever outside history or believing that, with guidance, she will attain the European standard of progress, both types of racism point out that the non-European is lacking. In the logic of racism, the European is complete while the Other is empty. The difference is in whether it is believed, as progressivists did, that this void can be filled, or whether it should merely be used until it is no longer useful and discarded, as the naturalist proponents of slavery had done. In the next chapter, we see how both types of racism have impacted upon and continue to shape the lived-experience of the racialized.

2
The experience of racism

What is left of the colonized at the end of this stubborn effort to dehumanize him? He is surely no longer an alter ego of the colonizer. He is hardly a human being. He tends rapidly towards becoming an object. As an end, in the colonizer's supreme ambition, he should exist only as a function of the needs of the colonizer, i.e., be transformed into a pure colonized.

Albert Memmi (1974: 130)

In the previous chapter, I focused on how racism develops as an idea; an idea strongly rooted in the intertwined histories of the West and of modernity. Racism has survived because of the centrality of the idea of race to the very ethos of the modern nation-state whose institutions govern us to this day. In this chapter, I ask how does racism work or, in other words, how is it translated from the political idea discussed in Chapter 1 into a complex system with direct effects on individuals' lives. Doing this should help us understand how and why racism continues today and lead us into the examination of some of the key manifestations of racism that make up the rest of this book.

The focus here is on the *experience* of racism. The notion of lived-experience will frequently be returned to. It was introduced by Frantz Fanon in his seminal work, *Black Skin, White Masks* which is discussed at greater length in the second part of this chapter. It is important to note that the English translation of the title of the fifth chapter misrepresents the author's meaning. The original French title – *L'experience vecue du noir* – literally, "the lived experience of the black man" – is translated into English as "The fact of blackness." This is a significant mistake that is bound up with the general problem we are faced with in this chapter. Rather than focusing on the problem of racism, all eyes are turned on the category of race specifically, and identity (national, ethnic, religious, etc.) more generally. Despite the efforts to deny that race has any real explanatory capacity and to prove that it is based on falsifiable pseudo-science, it continues to enthrall. The idea that there is a "fact of blackness" entirely misunderstands Fanon's point: that race is arbitrarily imposed on some by more powerful others. The "other" is raced – endowed with racial characteristics – while the white, the Western, and the colonizer remain race neutral, the standard against which the former is to be judged. Although it is important to refute the race concept on scientific grounds, what is of significance is not the fact of race itself but the process by which ra*cing* takes place. In other words, how does the experience of racism keep the idea of race afloat, both for the racialized and for those in a position of racial privilege, whether or not they actively believe that it objectively exists?

A recent example illustrates this point. The year 2007 marked the bicentenary of the Abolition of Slavery Act, passed by the British parliament in 1807. Debates around the commemorative events focused on the question of whether the descendants of African slaves should have the right to seek reparations for the damages of slavery. In a wider context, the very right of black people in general to feel personally affected by the history of slavery has been under discussion. The feeling among many commentators is that to blame the problems faced by black people today on the legacy of slavery, however difficult, is a step too far. For example, right-wing British commentator, Melanie Phillips, writing in the *Daily Mail* on March 26, 2007, ridicules the Bishop of Liverpool for drawing

> a link between slavery and the murder of black teenager Anthony Walker at the hands of racist thugs. The more he studied history, said the bishop, the more he believed "that our racism is rooted in the dehumanizing treatment of black people by white people."

For Phillips, it is inconceivable that the racism suffered by non-whites today could be perceived as being linked to a longer history of injustice, based on racist precepts going back to the "discovery" and colonization of what were thought of as uncharted territories by European explorers and their powerful benefactors.

However, the Bishop of Liverpool's analysis can be seen as central to the experiences of many black people. Despite the fact that slavery has been abolished and that the colonial chapter is officially closed, the same logic that enabled foreign domination and enslavement in colonial times continues to drive contemporary racism. It is how that logic – that non-whites are *lacking* in comparison to white Western people – is articulated that has changed, continually being transformed according to the political demands of the time. Today, at a time when it is considered that racism in its most vicious form is a thing of the past, what is most difficult for the majority within Western societies to accept is that racism continues to affect the lives of many people. As the example of the painful history of slavery makes clear, many are left wondering what all the fuss is about. It is this gap between what racism *is* and what many of us *think* it might be that will be addressed in order to begin to answer the question: how does racism function?

"The lived-experience of the black man"

Taking the title of Frantz Fanon's most influential chapter from *Black Skin, White Masks* as a guide, let us begin exploring how the complexities of these racisms affect people's lives. Once again, although it is racism as experience that we are concerned with here, it is from a political, and therefore a collective, point of view that I explore this, rather than from an individualized or psychological one.

As a psychiatrist, Fanon was interested in how racism and colonial domination affect the individual. However, the insights he offers in his best known writings, while drawing on his experience as a practitioner, are grounded in a commitment to radical societal change and are, therefore, fundamentally political. They are also collective because they resonate for oppressed people from a wide spectrum of backgrounds and geographical locations from Algiers to Alabama.

In his work, the distinction between the naturalist and historicist racism discussed in Chapter 1 becomes clear. Through reading Fanon we can also see the pernicious effect that the civilizing mission associated with the "progressive" attitudes of racial historicism has on societies and individuals. When Fanon arrived in France in the 1940s to study medicine, he was struck by an acute sense of the gap between the image of the "motherland" promoted by the French colonial education system, Martinican society, and the army, and the reality of his experience. Like countless numbers of colonial migrants, he saw France as his country and himself as a full citizen, protected by the universalist dictum of

THE CONTRIBUTION OF FRANTZ FANON

Frantz Fanon (1925–1961) was born on the French Antillean is-
land of Martinique. In 1944, he volunteered for the Free French
army. He believed that "his own freedom, that of Martinique and
that of France were inextricably bound up together" (Macey 2000:
91). However, his experience in France taught him that the French
did not share his conviction that Martinicans were equal citizens
of the "motherland." In 1946, Fanon nevertheless returned to
France to study medicine in Lyon, which was "notoriously un-
friendly to strangers" (ibid. 119). During his studies Fanon was
politically active and took part in anti-colonialist demonstrations.
He was influenced by philosophers such as Sartre and Merleau-
Ponty, and by African-American writing. This is reflected in *Black
Skin, White Masks*, his first book, published in 1952. Fanon began
to specialize in psychiatry.

   In 1953, he was posted to Algeria. In 1954, the Front de
Libération Nationale (FLN) embarked on a war of decolonization
against the French. Fanon's practice was in the town of Blida, known
as the "capital of madness." There he was made aware of the star-
tling differences between the manicured French neighborhoods and
the chaos of the Casbah: "Algeria transformed him into an advocate
of violent revolution" (ibid. 244). By 1955 he had contacts with the
FLN in Blida, and, by the end of 1956, he had been expelled from
Algeria and fled to Tunis, the FLN's capital in exile, where he continued to practice and to write for the FLN newspaper *El Moudjahid*.
By 1958 he was representing the Algerian cause abroad, mainly in
Sub-Saharan Africa. During this time, Fanon began to construct the
idea of the Algerian people based not on nationality but on the commitment to a future free Algerian nation. This contrasts with the reality that, despite Fanon's commitment to the Algerian cause, he
never became an official hero of the Algerian struggle for liberation.

   In 1961, suffering from the leukemia that was to claim his life,
Fanon wrote *The Wretched of the Earth*. The book became a veritable bible of anti-colonialism, influencing Third World revolutionaries and advocates of Black Power in the United States alike.
Fanon died in Washington on October 10, 1961.

liberté, égalité, fraternité. He was not the first to do so. Stuart Hall notes that the "Black Jacobin" Toussaint L'Ouverture, who fought to emancipate his fellow black slaves in the Haitian revolution (1791–1804), was influenced by the French revolution. As Hall reminds us:

> He was destined to be disappointed. "Les amis des noirs" at first emancipated only the "coloreds." Abolition was reluctantly extended to all slaves, but when Napoleon came to power, he revoked the edict and restored slavery. It was many decades later that slavery was eventually abolished in the French empire.

Fanon's shift from being a perfect product of progressivist education to becoming a radical opponent of colonialism in Algeria was undeniably sparked by his early realization of this gap between myth and reality. His realization prompted him in 1952 to write of the "lived-experience" of black people in the colonies. Lived-experience is fundamental to the explanation of racism because without listening to those who face the ill-treatment that results from racism, we are in no position to theorize it. The failure to put lived-experience at the center of many explanations of racism is the cause of the inadequacy of many theories of racism.

A key concept associated with Fanon's theorization of racism based on lived-experience is *racialization*. Racialization is vital for understanding how race is signified or, as Stuart Hall says, "made to mean." Just why does race take on the importance that it has over time? How is this translated into racism, experienced by individual people in everyday situations?

Racialization, as described in Fanon's work, consists of the processes of epidermilization, naturalization, and subjugation. Epidermilization is important in Fanon's work because of his focus on the experiences of black people. It refers to the relationship between skin color and the subjugation brought about by racism. It is common to think that racism is mainly about an objection to those with different (non-white) skin color. However, taking Fanon's ideas as a basis, we can see how visual signifiers other than skin color are also related to racism. A good contemporary example is the Muslim headscarf. With the rise in Islamophobia witnessed in the years following September 11, 2001, there has been a rise in racism against people perceived as being Muslim. Because many religious

Muslim women wear a headscarf (*hijab*) or face veil (*niqab*) they are recognizable as Muslim. Often accompanied by discourses about Muslim women as unemancipated, the headscarf or veil becomes a symbol for a host of negative attributes associated with Muslims generally.

These visual signifiers of racialized difference (skin color, dress, etc.) are intimately linked with the process of naturalization. In the case of the Muslim headscarf-wearing woman or the black-skinned person, they become reduced to that single aspect of their outward appearance. Even the headscarf, which can be taken off, is no longer seen as dissociable from an individual's character. It is seen as defining her entirely. Her whole being is reduced to that one aspect of her appearance. Moreover, her wearing of the veil is understood as being inseparable from her very nature. In this sense, she is naturalized.

Stuart Hall argues that naturalization is closely linked to fetishism, where we become transfixed by a particular aspect of, in this case a woman's, outward appearance. He cites the case of the "Hottentot," Saartje Baartman, brought to England in 1819 and exhibited at fairs and studied by scientists as an exemplary member of her "species." The public's fixation with Saartje's "difference" and, in particular, with certain parts of her body, led to her being symbolically dismantled. A collection of certain preserved parts of her body were even collected and displayed in the *Musée de l'Homme* in Paris. These parts were seen as enough to signify her whole being. Saartje had been turned into nothing but an object.

It becomes clear how racialization then is also about subjugation, because epidermilization and naturalization mean nothing in the absence of domination. It is only because racism developed within situations of exclusion and the exertion of power that it was able to function. The economic demands of colonialism and slavery required racial inequality to legitimize them. The position of power occupied by slave owners and colonizers could not but make them dominant over the "native." The imbalance of power between them meant not only that it took many decades for racism, slavery, and colonial domination to be challenged, but also that their legacies remain imprinted on future generations and in many ways continue to determine the nature of social and political relations in our post colonial societies.

How then is this threefold process of racialization developed within Frantz Fanon's unique account of the lived-experience of the colonized?

The opening lines of Chapter 5 alert us to the existence of "base" racism and how it is experienced as objectification through the use of traditional racist epithets. Fanon recounts a small child pointing him out to her mother and telling her she is frightened at the sight of him. He calls this common experience "crushing objecthood" (ibid.). He realizes that, as a black person, the only thing that is significant about him is the color of his skin. This is naturalist racism; one that sees non-whites as immutably other and therefore as a source of incredulity, ridicule or, in the case of the small child, fear. Fanon's aim in this chapter is essentially to search for a response to the feeling of objectification that he experiences on a daily basis on the street or "in the train [where] I was given not one, but two, three places" (ibid. 112).

His first reaction was to turn to what he instinctively saw as his legacy, not black consciousness or identity, but the Western intellectual tradition. Despite the denial of his selfhood that racism causes Fanon to experience, he attempts to rationalize it. He observes that "scientists had conceded that the Negro was a human being . . . the Negro had been proved analogous to the white man" (ibid. 119). However, as he quickly discovers, this does not ensure a change in his experience. As Fanon writes, "I had rationalized the world and the world had rejected me on the basis of color prejudice" (ibid. 123). In other words, he tried to use reason to make sense of the world around him, but he realizes that because he is a black man, what is expected of him is "unreason" (ibid.). In sum, despite the promises of equality that progressivism holds out to the colonized, Fanon's experiences reveal to him that, in reality, to be seen as fully capable of rational thought he would ultimately have to cease being black, and this is impossible. He thus realizes that he may never attain the full equality that had been promised to him.

Fanon's realization of the impossibility of his condition as neither fully French nor authentically black (he ultimately rejects the existence of authentic identity) is at the root of his analysis of the lived-experience of colonized people. He is concerned with how the "black person" is *brought into being*: an awareness of one's own skin has to be created. The fact of having black skin is not in itself significant for the individual whose skin is black; it is after all one's skin and is as such not perceived as being strange, different, or undesirable. The problem arises when black and white are brought into contact. The way in which they perceive each other is mediated by the uneven relationship of power that structures

DAYS OF GLORY

Fanon's experience is illustrated in the film *Days of Glory* (2006). The film tells the true story of a group of North African soldiers fighting in the French army during the Second World War, as did Fanon himself. Although the so-called "indigenous" soldiers, fighters from the French colonies from Senegal to Algeria to the Antilles, who saw it as their duty to defend the "motherland," made up the bulk of the French forces, they were the most ill-treated. The film catalogues the use of these troops as cannon fodder, as servants to higher ranking officers, and even the fact that they received less food than their white French counterparts. These inequalities were nonetheless accompanied by a discourse that promised the "indigenous" soldiers promotion and honor through military service. The film ends with the final few of the group still alive defending a village in Alsace against the Germans, having been promised that they would be the liberators of France, as the first French soldiers to go into Germany. With no troops sent to bolster their numbers, all but one of the remaining "indigenous" soldiers are massacred. Shortly after, French soldiers enter the village and are declared the liberators of France. Until the film was released, provoking an outrage, the French government had refused to pay the pensions of "indigenous" soldiers since the end of the war in 1945.

the colonial situation. This same imbalance of power also influences the interaction between "host" and "migrant" communities in post-colonial immigration societies today. As Fanon says, "as long as the black man is on his own, he will have no occasion, except in minor internal conflicts, to experience his being through others" (ibid. 109). But when black and white cohabit a space – the colonized land – the former begin to see themselves through the others' eyes. In fact, Fanon argues, because of the system of racial domination that underpins colonialism, it becomes impossible for the colonized to see themselves independently of the others' view of them.

For Fanon, the main effect that the lived-experience of colonialism and racism has on black people in the colonial situation is their internalization of the image that the colonizers have of them. An image, due to the centrality of racist beliefs about their assumed inferiority, that is damningly negative and often infantilizing. In practice this means that "not only must the black man be black; he must be black in relation to the white man" (ibid. 110). And this is a one-way street for, due to the inequality that divides them, the white person's identity is not determined by her black counterpart in the same way that the opposite is true. This is made clear when Fanon claims to have been "*fixed*," in the sense of having been essentialized, by "white eyes, the only real eyes" (ibid. 116). In other words, only whites have the authority to decide a person's identity and therefore her place in the world. This is echoed in Fanon's discussion of the relationship between the "native" and the "settler" in *The Wretched of the Earth* when he says, "it is the settler who has brought the native into existence and who perpetuates his existence" (2001: 28). In other words, the "native" is such only because she has been designated so by the settler. Likewise, a person's black skin is only significant insofar as it has been deemed undesirable according to a racial schema and linked to a condition of domination or inequality. The result of realizing the significance of one's own skin, and therefore one's difference from the white norm, for Fanon is a feeling of shame:

> Shame and self-contempt. Nausea. When people like me, they tell me it is in spite of my color. When they dislike me, they point out that it is not because of my color. Either way, I am locked into an infernal circle. (Fanon 1986: 116)

Fanon feels shame because he realizes that it *is* precisely his color that determines the reactions of others to him.

What are the consequences of this for the colonized? The experience of being only in relation to the other, of having been stripped of the capacity to define oneself, ranges from invisibility to dehumanization. As Goldberg, writing about Fanon, remarks, the reification of race, the fixing of non-white identities, leads to the dominated becoming invisible; because according to a racial vision of the world, whiteness is taken to be the norm or standard against which all must be judged, it casts a shadow over everything else, rendering it invisible. Visibility is associated with the positive attributes of access, opportunity, ability, and power. Invisibility is negative, standing for absence, lack, incapacity, and powerlessness. Visibility conveys whiteness – light and learning, while invisibility stands for blackness – darkness and degeneration.

> On these assumptions, visibility is taken as a virtue, a norm of whiteness amid the night of blackness. Visibility, then, should always be pursued, protected, cherished; invisibility is to be avoided, derided, denied. (Goldberg 1997: 81)

Causing the other to be invisible is based on a choice not to see her, or in other words, a choice not to recognize her significance or indeed her existence.

At worst, Fanon makes clear, what he calls the Manichean (dualistic, black and white) world of colonialism leads to the "native's" total dehumanization. In order for it to function, colonialism has to deny the colonized's ability to reason, to have ethics or values. This leads to the colonized being seen as a "corrosive element, destroying all that comes near him; he is the deforming element, disfiguring all that has to do with beauty or morality" (Fanon 2001: 32). This belief legitimizes the domination of the colonized and their lands, their exclusion, or indeed their killing. At its fullest expression, it "dehumanizes the native, or to speak plainly it turns him into an animal" (ibid.). The colonizers speak of "the yellow multitudes" or of the "black, brown and yellow masses which will soon be unleashed" (ibid. 33).

For Fanon, writing in *The Wretched of the Earth*, his call to arms against colonial domination, this dehumanization is at odds with progressivist attempts at instilling Western values in the colonized. He explains how "well-meaning souls" point out the "specificity and wealth of Western values" (ibid.). It is when the colonized realize the irony of appealing to the "native's reason" (ibid.) while referring to them as "hordes" and "hysterical masses" (ibid.) that they recognize their own humanity and come to see themselves independently for the first time.

Robert Young has criticized the dualism in Fanon and Albert Memmi, another important figure in the theorization of anti-colonialism and author of *The Colonizer and the Colonized*. He says that this view stresses separateness and constructs "two antithetical groups, the colonizer and the colonized, self and Other, with the second only knowable through a false representation, a Manichean division that threatens to reproduce the static, essentialist categories it seeks to undo" (Young 1995: 5). He proposes that the reality is more complex than this and that there has always been a great deal more "cultural contact, intrusion, fusion and disjunction" (ibid.) between peoples across the globe, especially in relations of sexual desire and intimacy.

While it is important to take note of Young's critique, it is also important for our purposes to understand the reasons for which the racially constructed world of the colonies could be experienced as unambiguously divided. Although intermixture and ambivalence about the certainty of race surely influenced the interaction between colonizer and colonized, the fact remains that admitting this would have been too destabilizing for the former. The system that structured colonial society was therefore officially based on this divide, a divide that perhaps because of its tenuousness in reality was profoundly important for explaining the condition of the colonized and of the racialized more widely. In other words, we must listen to accounts of the *experience* of racism in order to make sense of what racism is in reality and not just as an abstract concept. This is all the more important because, as we shall now see, race is much more about language and symbols than hard facts. If we want to understand how racism affects us we have to see how it plays out through processes of interaction, the institutionalization of a variety of practices and the use of symbols and discourses that often seem to be removed from the idea of biologically distinct races originally theorized by racial scientists.

Racism as a process of signification

The discussion of racism as lived-experience leads us inevitably back to the question of just where *race* is in all this? One might well ask, if racism is so important and has shaped so many people's lives in profound ways, as Fanon and others have shown us, how is it possible to argue that race does not exist? As I made clear in the introduction, race does not exist from a biological point of view, but it does exist from a sociological one. In other words, race has taken on a "life of its own" beyond any existence in fact. How can this be so? And what does it teach us about the experience of racism?

In 1997, a video transcript of a lecture delivered by the founder of British cultural studies, Stuart Hall, was made. *Race, the Floating Signifier* lays out Hall's position on the theoretical status of the idea of race. His insights, coupled with his views on stereotyping that we shall look at later on, help us to answer the questions posed above. Where does race itself come into the experience of racism? Hall argues that, rather than being an objectively provable category, race is a signifier. What does this mean? Linguistic theorists have divided the idea of a sign into two components: the signifier and the signified. The signifier is a representation. This can be a word, drawing, symbol (such as a road sign), or even body language. The signified on the other hand is the idea or object represented by the signifier. Therefore, race is a signifier that represents something else. This may conflict with the idea that many of us have that race is signified by other things, such as perhaps skin color, hair, or indeed intelligence or being good at sports! The opposite, argues Hall, is the case.

But why would we need a signifier like race? As I showed in Chapter 1, with the Enlightenment the need to classify everything in the world around us led gradually to the division of humankind into races. Despite the fact that the existence of actual races has been disputed, we still have a need for this classification. Hence, beyond the narrow confines of biologically determined categories, race has come over time to stand for (signify) a host of "differences," or ways of distinguishing between human beings.

Hall argues that race, like gender, works as a key signifier because of the fact that differences between people *do* exist. He argues against the extreme postmodernist position that claims that there are no actual differences and that any variations between individuals and groups are textual rather than real – because I say you are different, you are different. No, he says, people do look different from each other! "Differences exist in the world, but what matters are the systems of thought and language we use to make sense of the difference" (1997b). Race becomes a useful way of classifying people because, as we saw in the previous chapter, of its easy translation into the language of both science and politics. It is therefore easily harnessed to knowledge and power. In other words, it is easy to generate knowledge (facts) about differences that we term "racial" and use these facts to create and maintain systems of domination. This is clearly evident in the colonial situation Fanon writes about.

In essence, despite having been discredited as a scientifically useful form of classification, race retains an unusual power. As Hall remarks, "the biological definition [of race], having been shown out through the front door, tends to sidle around the veranda and crawl in the window" (ibid.). Although the way in which race impacts on our societies today is undeniably different from its effects during colonialism or slavery, it nonetheless endures. Indeed, a lot of the same fantasies and fears that legitimated racist regimes continue in subtle ways to determine the way in which we think of those who are different from us.

Race is still with us in myriad ways. Indeed, due to the extent that such myths and stereotypes are embedded in our language, they have become detached from their original source. Race quickly disappears between the lines to the extent that it becomes impossible to point out the racist origins of jokes and stereotypes because they are seen as a seamless part of language and, because language is fundamental to it, of culture. This is the nub of Hall's point in *Race, the Floating Signifier*. He claims that all attempts to define race have been in vain and this is because race is inherently discursive or, in other words, it "works like a language":

> Race is a signifier which can be linked to other signifiers in a representation. Its meaning is relational and it is constantly subject to redefinition in different cultures, different moments. There is always a certain sliding of meaning, always something left unsaid about race. Hence, race is a floating signifier. (1997b)

Let's unpack this claim. He argues that the signifier "race" is always related to an image or representation: the signified. In the case of race, what is signified is the image that we have of the human body and, in particular, the differences between human bodies. We use what he calls the "gross physical characteristics of color, hair and bone" (ibid.) as the visual representations of something unseen that we call race. Race is a shorthand for the intangible things about us, the things that make up who we are – things like "intelligence, morality, sexuality" (ibid.). Because we cannot see these things, we infer them on the basis of the visual representation – of a person's body – that we see in front of us. As Hall puts it:

> We read the body as a text. We inspect this text, the body. We are readers
> of race. We are readers of social difference. We invoke the body as if it
> were a transcendental signifier. (Ibid.)

These are things we all do. We look at people whom we don't know
and infer things about their personality on the basis of their appearance.
We may, for example, look at an overweight person and infer that they
are lazy, or at a handicapped person and presume that they feel sad. As
in the case of race, these are learned suppositions. It is because, for example, sixteenth-century Europeans had a worldview that saw blackness,
and therefore Africans, as the embodiment of satanic evil that they were
both fascinated and disgusted by black skin color. It is because being
physically different from the European "norm" has become associated
over time with a host of repellant and/or fetishized attributes, that we,
often unknowingly, continue to be guided by them in the way we react
to others. In the case of race, because physical characteristics have been
associated with unseen negative attributes (morality, intelligence, sexuality, etc.), the potential danger that this "otherness" poses to us has become controlled and accounted for. In other words, since early
European expansion overseas and the development of racial thinking
at home, as we saw in Chapter 1, difference has become increasingly
policed and bureaucratized. It therefore entered into our social con-
ventions. As the anthropologist Mary Douglas puts it:

> The human body is always treated as an image of society and
> . . . there can be no natural way of considering the body that does not at
> the same time involve a social dimension . . . If there is no concern to
> preserve social boundaries, I would not expect to find concern with
> bodily boundaries. (1970: 70)

The gut reaction that might lead one to cross the street at night when
we see a black man or group of men approaching us is related to how
the danger that we associate with otherness has entered into our way
of constructing images of insiders and outsiders. Race works as a means
of justifying, of lending legitimacy, to these fears of otherness, of
"strangeness." But it also creates and embellishes these fears. Because
there is a discourse that connects those who look different from our-
selves, who speak a different language or practice a different religion,

to the idea of a "threat," we may fear a certain group of people whether or not we have ever come into contact with them.

White fear of African-Americans demonstrates this. There are significant differences between being afraid and being in danger, but popular racism in the United States appears to function by making much of society believe that it has something to be afraid of: crime, violence, and drugs in particular. The result is that white people are taught to fear black people and that, as a consequence, black people fear the violence they may encounter as a reaction to the threat they are seen to pose. A Web article on the subject makes the point that:

> Many times we use stories to justify the fear that we feel toward people of color. We might introduce them by such phrases as "I was attacked once by ...," "I don't want to sound prejudiced, but I know someone who had a bad experience with ..." or "It's unfortunate, but my one negative experience was ..." We then use these single examples to reinforce a stereotype about a whole category of people and to prove the legitimacy of our fear of them.

Race, therefore, as a discourse or signifier, triggers fears, notions of threat, or even desires. It is this that makes it important. In other words, race is only significant because of the meaning it creates. This meaning has developed over time and may be transformed according to the era or the circumstance. In fact there is a whole *web of meaning* propping up our actions, our language and our thoughts that comes into play when we are confronted with the "strange." Without even knowing it, we are propelled towards certain thoughts and attitudes. This does not exonerate individuals who are overtly racist in their language or their actions. Rather, it reiterates the point that racism is not reducible to the attitude of an individual. It is rather the expression of a schema for making sense of otherness that, because of its success in infiltrating the very systems of thought that society as a whole draws on, needs to be challenged.

Much of what has been discussed above relates to the creation of *stereotypes* – generalizations or assumptions about people or groups of people. Hall distinguishes three functions of stereotyping. The first "reduces, essentializes, naturalizes and fixes 'difference'" (Hall 1997a: 258). This form of stereotyping is the fundamental object of Fanon's concerns in *Black Skin, White Masks*. Its second function is to divide between groups, or to distinguish the "normal and the acceptable from the abnormal and the unacceptable" (ibid.). It creates insiders and outsiders. This is largely what I have been suggesting is the purpose of race as a signifier. Third, they exist where there are imbalances of power, such as in the context of colonialism or in racially inequitable societies. In other words, stereotypes play a fundamental role in maintaining racism.

While stereotypes may have originated in social reality, they are constantly transformed and eventually take on a life of their own no matter how far from reality they depart. Nonetheless, "once formed, they assume certain features of a circular structure within which all behavior conforms to the internal directives of the stereotypical image" (Boskin and Dorinson 1985: 82). Stereotypes, then, are powerful. They have the ability to fix our view of others' behavior whether or not this is borne out in fact. To return to an earlier example, if we believe in the stereotype that all overweight people are lazy, we may find it difficult to believe that some suffer from a genetic disorder that causes them to be overweight.

The extent to which it is possible to contradict a stereotype and break the circular reasoning that it promotes depends, first, on the extent to which a stereotype is embedded in a society's culture, and second, the degree to which it is seen as useful to challenge a stereotype. Some stereotypes may simply maintain a status quo opinion useful for those with power in society. This should not be seen as assuming that Machiavellian reasoning is at play in the choice to maintain or destroy certain stereotypes. The processes involved are clearly much more complex and undoubtedly do not involve much overtly reasoned thinking. Politicians, for example, can often be heard to challenge a particular stereotype while actively promoting policies that keep it in place. A good example is the debate on immigration. While the majority of Western politicians today decry the existence of racism and even fund initiatives to combat it, in order to curb the numbers of "illegal immigrants" they participate in creating a stereotype of immigrants as "spongers" and even as criminals with potential terrorist links that do little to dispel common racist stereotypes. Stereotypes can be contradictory without this necessarily having any adverse effects on their potential to influence our way of thinking.

Let's look at the issue of racialized stereotypes a little more closely now by examining the racialization of female sexuality. Traditionally, there has been a double-edged relationship to the other's wholly imagined sexuality, a relationship that continues to this day. It is closely linked to the creation of stereotypes that often have damning effects, in particular on non-white and immigrant women (much of the stereotyping of Eastern European female migrants as prostitutes echoes more established ideas about black women). Racialized women have been seen as highly sexualized objects and as both sexually permissive and conservative in their behavior. How have these often contradictory views affected the way in which women in particular have experienced racism?

First, colonial fantasies created a two-sided image of the non-white woman, the first dominated by the African woman, or the black slave; the second by the Orientalist fantasy of the "Eastern" woman. Black women, like Saartje Baartman, were seen as savages, their nudity on constant display. They were therefore perceived as animal-like in their sexuality, voracious in their appetite for sex. It is clear how this image could be both a source of fear for Europeans, male and female alike, and of lust.

In contrast, the idea of Orientalism (Said 1978) that constructed the East as the fundamental opposite of the West, produced a different image of female sexuality. Orientalist fantasies saw the Eastern woman as highly desirable yet untouchable. The Oriental woman is seen as "mysterious, exotic and eroticized" (Hall 1997a: 260). However, because she is sold into marriage or perhaps veiled, and thus inaccessible to the European male gaze, she remains ethereal, an intangible idea. She becomes, therefore, both the object of intense fantasy and the epitome of the frigid female, rejecting the European male and thus disempowering and humiliating him. We can see how these Orientalist fantasies continue today with respect to the veiled Muslim woman. It is not uncommon to hear an objection to the veil that links it to sexuality. Not only are Muslim women seen as submissive, largely forced into wearing the veil by their fathers or husbands; in addition, veiling is seen as "unfair" because white women (my wife) can be seen by Muslim men, so why should the opposite not be the case? In other words, why are European men denied the possibility of looking at a Muslim woman unfettered by her veil?

The Seattle Public Library
Douglass-Truth Branch
Visit us on the Web: www.spl.org

Check out date: 12/13/15

xxxxxxxxx3642

Racism and ethnic bias : everybody's
0010043131928   Due date: 01/03/16
book

Racism and ethnic discrimination /
0010080097446   Due date: 01/03/16
book

TOTAL ITEMS: 2

Renewals: 206-386-4190
TeleCirc: 206-386-9015 / 24 hours a day
Online: myaccount.spl.org

* * * * * * * * * * * * * * * * * * * *
Pay your fines/fees online at pay.spl.org

How do sexualized stereotypes about non-white, non-Western women create a link between racism and sexism? Racism and sexism are clearly linked because they operate in similar ways. Because white males continue to be dominant within society, politics, and economics on a global level, patriarchy essentializes women in a way that bears sig-nificant resemblance to racialization. Whereas it is important to note that this does not exclude white women from racism, as the African-American scholar bell hooks reminds us, it does mean that racism against women has invariably been related to a sexualized male per-spective on female otherness.

The consequences of this are manifold, but two observations in par-ticular can be made. First, the non-white/non-Western woman is often painted as being sexually promiscuous, and even cast in the role of the prostitute, selling her body for money and, therefore, as amoral. Vednita Nelson, writing about the United States, claims that, racist stereotypes in the mainstream and entertainment media portray black women as sexually driven, promiscuous and indiscriminate. This image is further reinforced in the minds of white men because black neighborhoods are often zoned for businesses related to the sex industry Nelson argues that the reasons why some black women become prostitutes – poverty and deprivation and low educational qualifications – are generally ig-nored in mainstream analyses. In the US, slavery was a key time during which the image of black women as sexually promiscuous was gener-ated, because white masters could choose freely among the "slave girls" and impose sex on them.

Second, the consequence of the notion that black women are sex-ually promiscuous is that they are often treated unequally in rape cases and other situations of abuse such as domestic violence. Violence is commonly perceived as being part of the black household, with black males portrayed as aggressive and black women as permissive, often hav-ing children with multiple fathers. The subtext is that any violence meted out to them is earned, or at least inevitable.

Patricia Williams discusses the consequences of these attitudes for black female victims of crimes such as rape. She recalls the 1987 case of a black teenager, Tawana Brawley, found in an empty lot after disap-pearing for four days, almost naked and curled in the fetus position in a plastic bag with "KKK" and a racist epithet "inscribed on her torso; her body was smeared with dog feces" (Williams 2000: 423). Tawana claimed to have been repeatedly raped and beaten by three "white cops." As Williams describes it, the putting in motion of a media operation essentially to discredit Tawana, including referring to her as the "defendant" in the case, led to her claims being dismissed. In fact, it was concluded in court that she had made the story up: "Most people felt either that if she were raped it was 'consensual' (as cruel an oxymoron that ever was) or that she 'did it to herself'" (ibid.).

The kernel of this story, for Williams, is bound up with the stereotype of the black woman as a "whore." Because it is impossible to imagine white men actually desiring Tawana, she must comply with this stereotyped image. Williams distinguishes between prostitutes and whores. White women can become prostitutes under desperate circumstances. Black women, in contrast, are whores. It is, for them, "a way of being . . . Black women whore because it is sensual and lazy and vengeful. How can such a one be raped? Or so the story goes" (ibid. 426).

What Robert Young (1995) has called the "ambivalent movement of attraction and repulsion" sums up the relationship to the other's sexuality, both male and female. As we have seen, this form of stereotyping persists long after it became unacceptable to display the sexual organs of Saartje Baartman in a museum showcase. Nevertheless, when we consider the proliferation of pornography that fetishizes black or oriental sexuality and capitalizes on it (US$2.84 billion per year is made through Internet pornography alone), we can understand the extent to which these powerful stereotypes continue to frame sexual relations, and thus the highly racialized relations of power.

3

The lessons of antisemitism

It was my philosopher professor, a native of the Antilles, who recalled the fact to me one day: "Whenever you hear anyone abuse the Jews, pay attention because they are talking about you"... Later I realized that he meant, quite simply, an anti-Semite is inevitably anti-Negro.

Frantz Fanon (1986: 122)

So far I have dealt with the historical emergence of racism, as both a scientific concept, and more importantly, as a political idea, and with the effect it has when applied in concrete situations to the lives of ordinary people. The purpose of this chapter is to knit together the ideas of the first two chapters by looking at antisemitism. Why antisemitism, you may be thinking? Surely, in comparison with the racism experienced by migrants and asylum seekers and black and ethnic minority communities, Jews today are seldom the victims of either overt, violent or covert, institutionalized racism. Gone are the days when Jews were either openly threatened with persecution and genocide, or in other contexts, refused membership of clubs and ostracized by mainstream society. Some may argue that the shoe is on the other foot. Looking to the Middle East, it is Israeli Jews, some believe, who are now responsible for racist discrimination against another people: the Palestinians. In retaliation, others argue that anti-Zionism is just another form of racism in disguise. They point to the persistence of attacks against Jews and Jewish places of worship, schools, and monuments across Europe and, further afield, to the antisemitic attitudes of regimes in the Muslim world, in particular today in Ahmadinejad's Iran.

In short, antisemitism is still a hotly debated topic. This is because its legacy has a lot to teach us about the recent history of the Western world and, in particular, of Europe. In terms of racism itself, looking at the origins and development of antisemitism helps us to understand more clearly the ambivalent nature of racism.

In this chapter, my overall objective is to shed light on the idea that, although racisms are always multiple and context-specific, they nonetheless share fundamental characteristics. Indeed, all racisms are inherently internally multiple. In other words, they can each take different shapes at different times or places. As we shall see, antisemitism developed quite differently across various European countries in the nineteenth century. These differentiations and subtleties are common to all forms of racism. They all have the capacity to manifest themselves differently depending on when and where they arise. This should make it clear that, because of this variety, there is a great deal of commonalty between racisms against different people.

One of the greatest similarities is between antisemitism and present-day Islamophobia. As we shall see in Chapter 5 when we turn to the subject of racism in the context of the war on terror, the scapegoating of Muslims today mirrors that of Jews in the run-up to the Nazi Holocaust. That is not to say that the outcome will be the same. Merely, it points to the fact that racism invents and reinvents itself constantly under the conditions of modernity, nationalism, and capitalism. The parallel between antisemitism and Islamophobia is a good example of the importance of this observation for a deeper understanding of the phenomenon of racism.

In light of the above, this chapter looks at the relationship between antisemitism and racism, at the historical bases of modern antisemitism, and at the contemporary debate about the relationship often drawn between anti-Zionism and antisemitism. How does the conflation between the two obscure the similarities between different racisms and the potential solidarities that can be constructed in opposing them?

The flexibility of antisemitism

The term "antisemitism" was coined in 1879 by the German journalist Wilhelm Marr in a pamphlet entitled, "The Way to Victory of Germanicism over Judaism." In it he argued that the Jews were winning in a battle of the races against the German Aryans and that their dangerous influence could only be quelled if they were vanquished. The term introduced by Marr is wholly racial because it is based around the notion that the Jews are Semites and thus a race apart. Although the common spelling of the term is anti-Semitism, many scholars prefer to join the two words in recognition of the fact that antisemitism refers only to discrimination or hatred of the Jews. It is not leveled at any other "Semitic" peoples. Furthermore, taken alone, the word "Semitism" has no meaning. Therefore, the hyphenated anti-Semitism is not equivalent to anti-Americanism or anti-racism, for example. I use the joined up antisemitism to reflect a specific discourse targeting Jews that evolved within a precise historical period.

That period was the late nineteenth century and, in particular the 1880s, following the publication of Marr's pamphlet in Germany. Scholars such as Enzo Traverso have argued that while antisemitism in Germany was a society-wide phenomenon, its French variant mainly infected elites and the Church and was not present to as great an extent among the general public. Nonetheless, antisemitism in all its varieties could be found all over Europe, East and West, at this time, growing in force until the eruption of Nazism in the 1930s.

In the next section, I examine the conditions that made it possible for the Nazi genocide of the Jews, homosexuals, Gypsies, blacks, the handicapped, and other minorities to take place. Although the Nazi Holocaust, variably known as the *Shoah* or simply as Auschwitz, is mainly symbolized by the murder of six million Jews, many other groups were eradicated in a racist campaign that was not confined to the Jewish people. Indeed, an analysis of the processes that made Auschwitz possible sheds light on the similarities between racisms that the case of antisemitism makes clear. Before doing that, let us look at why antisemitism emerged at the time that it did. What were its principle characteristics? And what is its status as a racial theory? The answer to this last question helps us to understand how racism of all types borrows from a range of discourses to make its case.

From time immemorial, it seems, societies have mistrusted, ostracized, indeed *hated the Jews*. Since the birth of Christianity, the Jewish people were portrayed as the killers of Christ and thus guilty of the greatest possible crime. This hatred of the Jews can be traced back to the age of the Greeks and continued through the Roman era. In medieval Europe, ostracism of the Jews was formalized with many being denied entry into professions and confined to living in cramped ghettoes. The stereotypical antisemitic image of the "money-grabbing" Jew was immortalized by Shakespeare's Shylock in *The Merchant of Venice*. It originates in the fact that the Church during the Middle Ages forced Jews into the professions of accounting, rent collection, and money lending. They therefore became a source of hate and mistrust among the population from whom debts had to be collected. In 1492, the Alhambra Decree led to the expulsion of the Jews of Spain or to their obligatory conversion to Christianity. However, even conversion did not guarantee the Jews' safety. They were forced to renounce their religion and heritage through intermarriage with Catholics, or risk death.

The ancient origins of Jew-hatred are often used as an argument that antisemitism, and indeed racism in general, are age-old practices. However, it is important to note that the type of hatred practiced by the Church and spread among the population from ancient times was quite different to modern antisemitism. The ideology of antisemitism that developed at the end of the nineteenth century was unique. It differed from pre-modern Jew-hatred because of its basis in racial theory and the influence it had on nineteenth-century European politics. However, as we shall see, it continued to rely on a lot of the old myths of religiously inspired anti-Jewishness.

Old-fashioned Jew-hatred was propagated by the Christian Church. Jews were portrayed as having the blood of Christ on their hands. This was connected to the myth of Jews as blood-thirsty with a mission to destroy Christianity by means of the "blood libel." This was the so-called ritual murder of Gentile children whose blood, it was claimed, was used to make the unleavened bread eaten by Jews at Passover. Again, these myths have survived even today, a result of the success with which modern antisemitism made use of these age-old ideas for its own purposes. Despite the diabolical nature with which the Jews were perceived, leading to horrible acts being committed against them, Christian Jew-hatred was wholly different, if not less pernicious, in character from modern racial antisemitism. This is because Christian belief relied on the idea that the Jews were fundamental to the second coming of Christ. Quite simply, Christians believed that it was necessary to convert the Jews in order for Jesus Christ to return again, a fundamental part of Christian faith.

Today, many within the so-called Christian Right in the United States still hold these beliefs. They argue that the presence of the Jews in Israel facilitates the Second Coming. They have therefore formed powerful alliances with the Zionist right wing in Israel and the United States. Many argue that the power of the religious right-wing lobby in the United States stops the US administration from intervening to halt the disenfranchisement of the Palestinians.

The idea that Jews are necessary for the fulfillment of Christian aspirations was challenged by the emergence of antisemitism. Two theorists of this new ideology were Marr in Germany, and Drumont in France, author of a hugely influential book, *Jewish France* (1886). He argued that Jews and Aryans were two racially distinguishable groups. Nothing could be done to assimilate them. Drumont argued that there were ethnographical, psychological, and physiological factors that clearly distinguished the Jews as a separate group. Jews had become racialized. This meant that they could no longer be redeemed, either through conversion or by remaining apart from majority society, secluded in ghettoes. Their Jewishness was naturalized and, therefore could in no way be overcome. To use modern terminology, it was imprinted on their DNA.

Ideas taken from racial science that saw different groups as biologically and genetically different to each other were applied to the Jews. However, unlike in the case of non-white people, who looked very physically different from Europeans, in the case of the Jews, their assumed racial otherness was quite difficult to pin down. Jews went from being an excluded and hated cultural and religious minority to the dangerous "race within." Their invisibility led to a heightened paranoia that saw Jews and their influence everywhere. The fallacy of the racialization of the Jews is that it represented such a radical break from how they had been viewed before. Racism ensured that the Jews were beyond the redemption that Christian Jew-hatred permitted. Like naturalist racism, based on the developments in racial science, the logical consequence of antisemitism was that Aryans had to annihilate Jews or risk annihilation themselves in a veritable war that pitted race against race.

Antisemitism, however, was not just a theoretical variant of racial ideas, *but had its origins in politics*. Just as anti-black racism was developed to argue that black people in the colonies were inferior to whites, antisemitism had a political purpose. It is essential to remember that anti-black racism and antisemitism were developed at the same time. The first legitimated the destruction caused by imperialism and colonialism in the "new world"; the latter sought to explain the turmoil that modernity brought to society at home.

In late nineteenth-century Europe, Jews were essentially the scapegoats that non-white immigrants were later to become following the end of the Second World War. Enzo Traverso proposes that antisemitism can be seen as a kind of cultural code. In other words, the Jews came to stand for everything that was wrong in society. From whatever point of view, left or right of the political spectrum, committed Christian or avowed secularist, it was possible to find an explanation for society's problems by looking to the Jews. The reasons for this should be seen in the context of nationalism that, as we saw in Chapter 1, is intimately related to the development of racism. The Jewish people had always been seen according to the stereotype of the "wandering Jew," a group without a homeland, with no essential identification with any place. This was before the Zionist movement and the eventual birth of the State of Israel created a nationalism for the Jews. Before European nationalism influenced Jewish people to claim their own place within the "family of nations," the land of Israel was a mythical place connected to the religious Messianism of the Jewish faith. It was certainly not a place that many diaspora Jews envisaged living in!

This "wandering Jew," therefore, increasingly became seen as threatening within the context of developing nationalism. As Enzo Traverso remarks, from the point of view of nation-building, the existence of the Jews served as a unifying factor. The Romantic nationalists' aim of erasing the universal humanism of the Enlightenment, opposed the idea that it was possible for a people to be without a nation. It was necessary to refute this idea in order to convince people of the attractiveness, indeed the necessity, of living together within nations. The cosmopolitanism of the Jews was seen as fundamentally threatening. Linked to a parallel discourse about the Jews as powerful manipulators of finance and wealth, and as controllers of the means of propaganda through their involvement in the press and education, nationalism saw the Jews as the natural enemy of the nation. The power of antisemitism within the nationalist movement supports the view that the ideas of race and nation are closely related. From a nationalistic perspective, Jews were seen as a nation apart. Because they nevertheless lived among other nations, they were seen as imposters and as eternal outsiders. Nationalism, like racism, saw the nation as organic and natural; the idea that one could swap nationalities and assimilate into the "host" nation was as inconceivable as a white man becoming black.

Within the demands of nationalism, antisemitism had a further purpose to fulfill in the late 1800s. As we saw in Chapter 1, the political usages of racism were indissociable from the personal destinies of whole groups of people within French and German societies, where much of the debate was centered. Aristocrats and would-be nobles, such as Arthur de Gobineau, as well as the Church and the right wing, saw nationalism as a means of countering the danger posed by the cosmopolitan aspirations of the Enlightenment. Racism and the specific ideas of antisemitism were used as arguments for building strong "race nations" that could resist infiltration from the Jewish "enemy within." Jews were seen as having too much wealth and power despite the fact that the majority were clearly far from being either wealthy or powerful. Nonetheless, their influence was imagined everywhere; in both rapacious capitalism and subversive Marxism, as both robbers and revolutionaries. The decline of the power of the aristocracy as well as the growing secularism of society needed to be blamed on someone if the two main groups affected – the aristocracy and the Church – were to claw back some of their power. A marriage of ancient Jew-hatred and the new science of race became the perfect way to blame the ills of modern life on the eternal outsider.

We can see how antisemitism could be so evocative. Antisemitism was not a purely scientific theory. It did not rely on cranial measurements and all the other strange procedures of racial science, although it was surely open to them. Rather, from the start, antisemitism was a political movement that *used* racial ideas, rather than the other way round. While race began as a scientific concept that developed politically due to its marriage with nationalism, antisemitism was wholly ideological. The significance of this observation is that, from the outset, antisemitism was built upon a mixed bag of ideas that, scrambled together, could be made into a convincing argument about the danger posed by the Jews.

Antisemitism, therefore, is proof that, as Robert Young (1995: 28) puts it, "the racial was always cultural." What is meant by this? As we shall see in the next chapter when we discuss the idea of a new "culturalist" racism, race and culture are two sides of the same coin or, as Young puts it, they develop together. Quite simply, it is just as easy to essentialize someone's physical characteristics (i.e. skin color) as it is to essentialize their culture (i.e. Judaism). As we saw in Chapter 2, it is the process of making this facet of a person's character fixed, unchanging, and natural that is what we call racialization. The linking

THE *PROTOCOLS OF THE ELDERS OF ZION*

The forged pamphlet known as the *Protocols of the Elders of Zion* is the best-known example of antisemitic propaganda. The twenty-four "Protocols" are said to be instructions to a new elder on how to trick gentiles in order to bring about Jewish world domination. Their themes reveal the conservatism of the Protocols' writers, most probably the Russian secret services. For example, one of the protocols advocates spreading as many conflicting ideologies as possible, including Marxism, Darwinism, Nietzsche-ism, liberalism, socialism, and more. Also emphasized are universal suffrage, world government, materialism, and economic depressions, as well as pornography. The worst fears of right-wing reactionaries – that Jews were responsible for bringing these unwanted changes into society – were behind the writing of the Protocols. The success of the *Protocols of the Elders of Zion* was in its ability to be internationally relevant. Facts and dates are skimmed over, allowing it to be used in a variety of contexts and times. It has been published all over Europe, East and West, apartheid South Africa, North America, and the Middle East. It was widely propagated by the Nazi regime. The fact that the pamphlet was said to have been written by Jews adds to its perceived legitimacy. It lends weight to the idea that the Jews were everywhere, controlling every force in society with the sole objective of destroying the Aryan race and the Christian people. Henry Ford, whose newspaper published the Protocols, claimed in an interview in 1921 that, "the only statement I care to make about the Protocols is that they fit in with what is going on." Today, despite having been officially renounced as a forgery by *The Times* of London as early as 1921, the Protocols continue to be popular among the far right. For example, among the 603,000 Google hits for "The Protocols of Zion," a Web site called JewWatch.com states, in reference to the Protocols, that "the Jews are at the top, the ones who are conspirators against all of mankind today and always have gained power and maintain it through world domination and control of all means of communication."

of scientific ideas about racial categorization to the realities of what we see in society – that people are different – and the use of such discourses within the context of political challenges such as nation-building, encapsulates the politics of race and racism.

What were the different arguments – racial, cultural, and political – used by antisemitic movements to make their case? MacMaster claims that ideological antisemitism drew on five main themes. These filtered down into society with profound social and political effects. Although pre-modern ideas that bore resemblance to antisemitism were already widespread in society, it took the formation of actual movements to promote an antisemitic agenda to make modern antisemitism as significant for European society as it became in the years following 1880. The five themes MacMaster lists are economy, religion, degeneration, nationalism, and science. I have already demonstrated how nationalism and religion were important for the development of ideological antisemitism. How did these relate to the remaining three themes?

The five strands within ideological antisemitism become powerful discourses because of the ability of each to draw on age-old anti-Jewish ideas and connect them to the newer notions that came from racism and nationalism. *Economic antisemitism* drew on the prevalent view of Jews as the exploiters of hard-working Christians that had existed since their confinement to the role of money-lending. In the modern context, Jews were seen as holding the purse strings of finance capitalism and modern banking. Jewish bankers like the Rothschilds were targets of particular hatred and attacked by conservatives and Marxists, both of whom were opposed to the accumulation of great personal wealth. Antisemitism drew on the anti-capitalism of Marxism, but unlike it, saw the Jews, rather than the bourgeoisie and the modern state structure, as responsible for the inequalities of capitalist systems. The few rich Jews who were indeed able to access the upper echelons of society in post-emancipation Europe were a scapegoat for the frustrations of those who lost out due to modernization and the spread of capitalism.

Ironically, however, opponents of Marxism, in particular the aristocracy, landowners, and the wealthy in general, also saw the Jew as the fomenter of revolution. Far from being capitalists par excellence, Jews were responsible for the threat from international Socialism or Communism. Many Jews were indeed attracted to the ideas of Socialism and were committed Marxists. For the opponents of Marxism, fearful of the very real threat of the revolution that eventually overthrew the Czar in Russia in 1917, the cosmopolitanism of the Jews made them the epitome of the revolutionary. It was believed that the Jews, having no nation of their own, would be happy to see that of others overthrown, and the order of the world, formed of races and nations each in its place, destroyed.

MacMaster argues that the incoherency of these two opposing views that saw Jews as the agents of both capitalism and anti-capitalism was irrelevant to the success of antisemitism. People were looking for a totalizing and holistic explanation for the problems of society at what was a particularly turbulent time, full of change and uncertainty. The existence of the Jews in society functioned as an explanation of all society's ills. It resolved all apparent contradictions.

Parallels can be made to the debate on immigration in Western societies today. The figures frequently quoted by anti-immigration lobbyists and the right-wing press on the numbers of immigrants are often preposterous. For example, in Britain in 2007 the debate about the accession of Bulgaria and Romania to the European Union sparked fierce debate as to the numbers of economic migrants who would travel to seek work in the UK. A headline in the right-wing *Daily Mail* newspaper on April 26, 2007, reads, "Migrant numbers triple from new EU countries." The article goes on to state that "Figures today show 60,000 citizens from the two Eastern European countries arrived in Britain in the three months to February, compared with 23,000 for the same period in 2005/06." However, on closer examination, it can be found that the figures cited were actually drawn from a report on the numbers of visitors, including tourists, visiting the UK in that period, rather than the number of migrant workers alone. The point is that the lack of mathematical precision is of little importance to a reader who wants to believe that what the newspaper is stating is the truth. Likewise, the ridiculousness of the idea that an international conspiracy of Jews in the nineteenth century could bring about the "triumph or ruin of a government, an institution, an enterprise, or a man" (Winock 1998, cited in MacMaster 2001: 88) does not belie the fact that there were many who believed that this was in fact the truth.

Apart from the Christian myths about Jews as the killers of Christ and about their subversive power in the economic field, Jews were portrayed as dangerous for the very survival of the white, European race.

Racial ideas served to free ideological antisemitism from the confines of religious anti-Jewish mythology. In an age when religion, although far from being rejected, was being challenged by science, race was seen as a more solid explanation of the danger of the Jews.

In the nineteenth century, the influence of the racial science of Gobineau and others created a moral panic about *racial degeneration* that was mixed up with fears about the spread of disease. Syphilis in particular was seen as a great threat, clearly demonstrating how fears about contamination were mixed up with anxieties about sexuality. Miscegenation – the mixing of races that was seen as leading to "bastardization" and racial "impurity" – was a great fear. Jews were seen as the carriers of disease and dangerous germs that could infect European society. But they were also seen as responsible for the, mainly mythical, white slave trade and as the organizers of prostitution. The Jews were therefore believed to be plotting the downfall of the European races by mixing their blood with that of inferiors. As MacMaster comments, the "nebulous" idea of degeneration was mixed up with Europeans' fears about health, sexuality, and morality. It is easy to see how the Jews were a scapegoat for justifying the Europeans' own guilt about both sex with prostitutes at home and interracial intercourse with non-whites in the colonies.

The idea that the Jews were pathological fomenters of physical destruction on a mission to weaken and perhaps exterminate the European race was a powerful one. The image of the Jew as both diseased and evil dominated the caricatures that ideological antisemites used to propagate their message. Although many Jews in the urban centers of Europe were assimilated, the caricatured Jew wore the caftan, locks, and stereotypical hooked nose of the religious Jews of Eastern Europe. This image was captured by Charles Dickens in his portrayal of Fagin in *Oliver Twist*, an old man ravaged by disfigurement, with a rabid hunger for money, who enslaves white children to do his bidding.

Although the assimilated Jews were much more hated than Orthodox Jews, it was the latter's image that worked in antisemitic propaganda. Racial antisemitism worked with this caricature of the Jew and gave it scientific backing. The idea put forward was that no matter how like his countrymen the assimilated Jew looked, he or she was always a "real" Jew underneath. Biology, it was said, gave the lie to clever disguises. The Jew was a Jew on the inside and this is what really counted. Hence, popular antisemitic propaganda used tales of assimilated Jews, indistinguishable from Europeans, suddenly transmogrifying into their "real" selves, becoming "deformed and twisted, bow-legged and diseased, [with] thick black locks, fleshy lips, a hooked nose" (MacMaster 2001: 97). The moral of the story is that race is the most powerful identifier. Although racial markers can remain hidden for years – especially by the sly and manipulative Jew – they cannot forever remain obscured. It is up to Europeans to be on their guard!

The power of racial science as an apparent means of proving the essential difference of the Jews and the danger they posed to the survival of the Europeans is undeniable. However, it did not function alone. Ideas of race were supported by caricaturing images that spelled out the Jews' true essence in visual form: the hooked-nosed, bent, and monstrous-looking man who also featured in Christian Jew-hatred. Moreover, modern-day political concerns about the economy and the three-way split between cosmopolitanism, nationalism, and Marxism were also thrown into the mix. Ideological antisemitism was, therefore, a mixed bag of referents, images, and ideas. It used ideas about culture, politics, and economics as well as the ideas of racial science to make the point that the Jews were undesirable.

This ambivalence about the message actually being promoted by antisemitism is important. The example of modern antisemitism proves that race, rather than being a fact, is a signifier that symbolizes its underlying meaning. The most important thing that is retained from the original idea of race, and the reason why it continues to be so important today, is the idea of fixity. Race, for the first time, introduces the idea that a person's or group's character cannot change because it is part of who they are; it is natural. However, through a series of twists and turns, the element that is fixed shifts and can be associated with different facets of that group's characteristics, be they cultural or biological.

During the Nazi regime, for example, even people with only one Jewish grandparent, known as *Mischlings*, were considered Jews on some level, and many were sent to their deaths. A similar principle applied to the "one-drop rule" in the segregated United States that stated that anybody with some black ancestry was, for all intents and purposes, black. These laws acted on the fear of racial impurity brought about by miscegenation. However, the reverse principle was never applied: that if a person had only one Jewish ancestor, they were in fact more Christian than they were Jewish. When thought about from this point of view, it is clear that racial notions of purity are bogus. They have therefore always relied on accompanying discourses (religion, politics, economics, etc.) but also on a particular structure of power in which to operate. It is when power arrangements in society make it possible for the dominant group to discriminate against a minority that racism comes to the fore.

Antisemitism and modernity

In Chapter 1, I argued that racism, far from being age-old, is a feature of modernity. Let us return to that argument now by looking at the specific case of antisemitism. In the European context it was the particular pressures brought about by modern life that enabled antisemitism as a movement to grow. Understanding the uniqueness of these modern pressures helps us, in turn, to understand the development of racism and antisemitism.

Antisemitic movements, like anti-immigration lobbies today, were reacting to change in society. Essentially conservative and mistrustful of progress, the antisemites were also wary of modernization, urbanization, and their cultural spin-off, cosmopolitanism. Just as the far right-wing today in an era of globalization links migration to a loss of traditional national values, so the antisemites saw the Jews as responsible for the rapid political, economic, and social changes that were leaving them behind. Some of those being left behind, as we have seen, were religious groups and the aristocracy. But it was also easy to appeal to an artisan class that was clearly losing out due to greater industrialization. Contemporary parallels can be made to a white working class losing jobs in an era of transnational manufacturing. It is often easier to blame migrants for "taking jobs" than to rationalize the complex reality of economic globalization that leads to jobs being lost to poor migrants at home and sweatshop workers abroad.

For the nineteenth-century antisemites, however, the problem was not only economic. Indeed, it could be argued that the antisemitic ideologues were more concerned with a cultural change in society that they attributed to the Jews. The Jews' status as a "nation within a nation" meant that they could not be trusted. They would never bear full allegiance to the nation. This was seen as being proven by Jewish involvement in finance capital and international socialism, and their cosmopolitan lifestyles, although these are stereotypes in themselves: only a minority of Jews actually led such interesting lives! Significantly, the picture evoked here has little to do with the caftan-wearing, hooked-nosed, and bearded Jew of the caricatures. And this is the core of the problem. In fact, the antisemitic movements in Germany, France, and the urban centers of Eastern Europe did not have much of a problem with these Jews, far away in their rural *shtetls* or ghettoized urban communities. The type of Jew feared and reviled by the antisemites was the assimilated Jew who looked and acted no differently from his European neighbor. Why was this the case?

Several influential scholars of antisemitism and racism, such as the German philosopher, Hannah Arendt, and the Polish sociologist, Zygmunt Bauman, have argued that antisemitism must be understood in the context of Jewish emancipation. Although it may appear extremely ironic, antisemitism – like racism in general – grew at a time of unparalleled equality when European societies were moving towards greater democracy. To understand antisemitism in the context of modernity, it is necessary to make sense of this paradox.

The Jews of Europe were emancipated between the late eighteenth century and the mid nineteenth-century, first in France after the French revolution and, by 1848 in Germany. Before this time, they lived under the control of the state, confined to certain areas and professions. They were not full citizens and were denied the right to vote. The spirit of the French revolution changed that. Based on the belief that all people should be free and equal, the Jacobins went about emancipating the Jews of France. The same democratization later spread throughout the rest of Western Europe. However, Jewish emancipation came at a price, particularly in the bloody aftermath of the French revolution.

The period of the Jacobin-led "terror," following the 1789 revolution in France, was dramatic for many religious followers whose beliefs were opposed to the secularism of the revolutionaries. Many of the Christian faithful lost their lives. Religious Jews were in a perilous situation. Unlike the mainly Sephardic Jews of southern France, many of whom were secularized tradespeople, the Ashkenazi Orthodox Jews of Alsace in the north were stunned by the demands of emancipation. As a consequence of being emancipated, the Jews were forced to relinquish their religious way of life, for it went against the secular culture that the Jacobins sought to instill. Synagogues and rabbinical schools were closed down and ritual slaughter and the celebration of Shabbat (Sabbath) were outlawed. This was the price to be paid for emancipation. For the Orthodox Jews who had lived a separate life, unfettered by the majority, emancipation did not mean freedom; it meant their way of life had been erased. It was a cruel irony. Becoming a citizen meant no longer being a Jew. Emancipation was therefore a top-down process, an "enlightened despotism" (Traverso 1996: 15). The Jews themselves neither asked for it nor played any role in defining what it would mean for them. The emancipation of the Jews of France turned Jews into individuals and, in the process, it threatened the continued existence of the Jews as a community.

Traverso contrasts Jewish emancipation under the Jacobins with the later emancipation of the Jews of Germany following the revolution of 1848. The French saw emancipation as part of an abstract commitment to humanitarian principles that were bound up with the values of nationalism, as opposed to the reign of the monarchy. The Germans, in contrast, saw emancipation more in terms of tolerance or of civic acceptance and related it to the principle of naturalization more generally. In other words, the Germans referred less to the lofty values that drove the French to free the Jews. However, the result for the Jews themselves was in effect the same. Both assimilated and religious Jews were at best tolerated, at worst mistrusted. It could well be argued that the origins of their exclusion can be found in their absence from the process of emancipation. Had Jews been the agents of their own emancipation, there may have been less of a tendency to see them either as eternally indebted to the "host" nation or ungrateful for their elevated position in society. In reality, they were doomed to be seen as one or the other, or both. Jews were either too ingratiating or too exclusionary. In other words, they could never be "one of us."

This image of the Jews as being either subservient or ungrateful is at the core of Hannah Arendt's explanation of modern antisemitism. In her highly influential book, *The Origins of Totalitarianism*, Arendt examined the roots of modern antisemitism in Germany and France. She claims that the antisemitic movements that emerged during the 1880s were spurred on by ambivalence towards assimilated Jews. Since the period of emancipation, Jews who chose to become assimilated, either for survival or out of choice, were regarded with mistrust. She explains that being Jewish was not seen in religious terms, or even only in cultural or racial terms. It came to be seen as a psychological quality.

Arendt distinguishes between Judaism and Jewishness. Assimilated Jews, especially the urbanized and educated, wanted to no longer be seen as Jews but only as members of the nation. However, while it was easy to erase one's Judaism by converting or relinquishing a Jewish way of life, the essence of one's Jewishness could never be gotten rid of. The totalizing effect of race ensured this. Jews, therefore, were seen as either "pariahs" or "parvenus." If they kept their traditions they were "untouchables," outside mainstream society. However, if they embraced the nation and forgot Judaism they were imposters, who could no more be German or French than a Chinese or an Indian person could.

Zygmunt Bauman describes this situation as a trap. If Jews refused to assimilate, they were condemned to living eternally as strangers within their own countries. If, on the other hand, they did assimilate as so many did, they were justifying the claim that Aryans were indeed superior to Jews. By rushing to become like their co-nationals, Jews were effectively complying with the idea that the Jewish "race" was inferior. They were trapped within a vicious circle. The more Jews assimilated, the less they could rely on a Jewish community to protect them. Quite simply, in Germany in particular, the traditional observant Jewish community was all but eroded.

Yet, although many Jews became completely assimilated, indistinguishable in every way from any fellow citizen, their very Germanness or Frenchness was seen as suspect. What were the Jews trying to prove? The feeling was that there had to be a reason for the Jews to want so desperately to be like the majority. Allied to ideas about Jewish involvement in subversion, from either capitalist or communist quarters, or both, it is easy to see how a general paranoia about the Jews was able to grow.

Ideological antisemitism played on this paranoia that saw Jews everywhere. Where did this seemingly irrational perception come from?

Hannah Arendt controversially argued in *The Origins of Totalitarianism* that the Jews could not be seen to have played no part at all in the growth of mistrust that surrounded them. This goes against the dominant opinion among scholars of antisemitism that tends to see the Jews purely as victims. Whereas it would be wrong to apportion blame, some have suggested that failing to admit that a minority of Jews played a

THE DREYFUS AFFAIR

Assimilated Jews in France at the end of the nineteenth century were not excluded from public life, and some even enjoyed relatively important positions. A promising young captain in the French army, Alfred Dreyfus, was an example. In 1894 he was abruptly arrested and accused of passing military secrets to the Germans, charged with treason, and imprisoned in exile. The evidence against Dreyfus was virtually non-existent. However, by the time this was realized, he had already been convicted and the army feared that a retraction would prove unpopular among the right wing. Antisemitic newspapers such as *Libre parole* cited the Dreyfus Affair as an example of Jewish treachery. Despite this, two years after Dreyfus's conviction, the new chief of army intelligence, Lieutenant Colonel Georges Picquart, ironically himself an avowed antisemite, found that the guilty party was in fact a Major Walsin Esterhazy. Picquart soon discovered, however, that the army was more concerned with preserving its image than rectifying its error, and when he persisted in attempting to reopen the case the army transferred him to Tunisia. A military court then acquitted Esterhazy. Nevertheless, the writer Emile Zola, in his famous open letter, *J'accuse*, attempted to have Dreyfus absolved of guilt. It was in vain, as Zola himself was accused of libel by the army and forced to flee. Public opinion generally condemned Dreyfus. It was influenced by the political right and the leadership of the Catholic Church who declared the Dreyfus case to be a conspiracy of Jews and Freemasons set on damaging the prestige of the army and destroying France. In 1899 the army again court-martialed Dreyfus. He was again found guilty and sentenced to ten years' detention, although it was observed that there were "extenuating circumstances." In September 1899, the president of France pardoned Dreyfus, thereby making it possible for him to return to Paris, but he had to wait until 1906 to be exonerated of the charges and restored to his former military rank. Although the Dreyfus Affair mobilized socialists, radicals, and republicans to work together against the right wing and the Catholic Church who promoted an antisemitic agenda, it fuelled a society-wide obsession with Jews.

part in their own unpopularity would be to paint all Jews as weak scapegoats. Scott Handlemann argues that the refusal of accounts of political antisemitism to deal with precise historical facts about aspects of the Jews' behavior is a denial of the prime significance of human agency. In other words, people, not abstract processes, are always responsible for the way events occur.

Arendt shows that because of the Jews' situation prior to emancipation, they allied themselves to whatever regime happened to hold power as a means of protecting themselves. Because of their position in the world of finance, which had evolved over centuries, leading to a minority of Jews becoming extremely rich and powerful, their fortune clearly lay with that of the state and vice versa. Arendt notes that, because of their direct relationship with the state prior to emancipation, most Jews found themselves outside all social classes, with no allies within civil society. Once the nation-state had become established, Jews could no longer be assured of this relationship. Paradoxically, the republican drive to create a fairer society that challenged rule by the nobility also disenfranchised Jews who enjoyed the protection of kings. Only a minority among them continued to benefit from a special relationship with the state, a fact that was openly resented. Financially powerful Jewish families, such as the Rothschilds since the time of Napoleon in France or the Warburgs in Germany after the First World War, quickly shifted allegiances according to the flow of power. Arendt notes that "each class of society which came into conflict with the state as such became anti-Semitic because the only social group which seemed to represent the state were the Jews" (cited in Handleman 2003: 17).

The point, therefore, is that the growth of antisemitism must be understood within the political context out of which it evolved. Seeing the Jews as agents of these political circumstances does not diminish the significance of the antisemitism that was waged against them. However, the significance of stereotypes discussed in the previous chapter should be borne in mind. For every powerful Jewish family whose political machinations may have fuelled anti-Jewish sentiment, there were tens of thousands of ordinary families who had no such involvement. The power of antisemitism, and racial stereotypes in general, is in its ability to distort and exaggerate a kernel of truth, decontextualizing it beyond recognition.

The process that led to the unleashing of ideological antisemitism followed the shifts in the Jews' condition following the French revolution and peaked after the revolutions of 1848. Antisemitism developed as a movement in the late nineteenth century after Jews had been emancipated in France for almost a century and in Germany for almost half that. Added to the resentment against the powerful Jews and their role as the state's bankers, ordinary Jews were targeted because of the drive to assimilate that accompanied emancipation. Here most Jews had little influence over their treatment. For many among them, as far as they were concerned, emancipation had allowed them full membership of the nation, and that was all that interested them. They wanted to behave like anyone else, and to be treated the same in return. The problem, however, was precisely the fact that Jews had become like their co-nationals. They looked like them, dressed the same way, and spoke the same language. Whereas before emancipation, Jews could be easily distinguished and thus kept in their place, the growing homogenization of society since emancipation had destroyed the old certainties that came with having clearly separated insiders and outsiders.

Zygmunt Bauman explains that before emancipation the Jewish condition was seen as "natural" whereas, following their assimilation, their situation became much more artificial. What is meant by this? Bauman introduces a useful analogy to help understand the problem of modern antisemitism. He compares the organization of society prior to Jewish emancipation to gamekeeping. The gamekeeper does not have to worry about planning like the gardener does. The rulers of pre-modern society could let things take their course, assured that society would take care of itself. The social divisions into classes, castes, religions, etc., meant that each was self-governing. Rulers only had to ensure that general order was kept. In this scheme, the Jews in their ghettoes and *shtetls* kept themselves to themselves. Knowing that they could not overstep the mark without great risk, they paid their taxes and organized themselves internally. They were a burden to no one. The fact that the Jews were different was of no concern. They could live as they wanted as long as they didn't impinge on anyone else. No doubt Christians hated and perhaps even feared Jews, and certainly many Jews suffered as a result. But they were not seen as a general threat to society in the way that they were following 1880.

Why does this change? Bauman argues that it is impossible to explain antisemitism and racism without understanding the overall changes that came about as a consequence of modernity. This includes industrialization, urbanization, growing secularism, and the idea of nationalism, rather than the small-scale community, as a social glue. For society to function under the conditions of modernity, mere gamekeeping becomes insufficient. It is not enough for rulers to sit back and let society organize itself, content only with taking taxes and otherwise leaving communities to their own devices.

The modern ruler is more like a gardener. As in the modern garden, so in modern society everything now had its place. As Bauman puts it:

> Nothing should grow unless planted, and whatever would have grown on its own must have been the wrong thing, and hence a dangerous thing, jeopardizing or confounding the overall plan. (1989: 57)

Just as the gardener uses herbicides to kill weeds, so too modern rulers were armed with the means to get rid of those who did not conform to the overall plan for society. It is not coincidental that modern, symmetrical gardens such as the *Jardins des Tuileries* in Paris did not exist before the seventeenth century. There was simply no conception that nature should or could be ordered in such a way before. For Bauman, it is the logic symbolized by gardening that enables the Nazi genocide to occur. It is not that the Germans were particularly disposed to antisemitism, as some have claimed. It can be argued that the antisemitic movement did perhaps find a stronger foothold in Germany than it did elsewhere, but this was due to societal pressures such as the political and economic failures that led to Germany's defeat in the First World War. He argues against the idea of German exceptionalism. On the contrary, he claims that there was something distinctive about the way in which modern nation-states in general evolved in the West, as increasingly competitive, expansionist, and bureaucratic, that sowed the seeds for the atrocities of the Holocaust and, I would add, colonialism.

The modern state, therefore, needs tools such as demography and statistics to know its population, so as to be able to ensure order in society. This was particularly important under the conditions of assimilation. Emancipation of the Jews led to the situation in which it was simply impossible to know instinctively who was who. Keeping in mind that the idea that "race is all" was at its height at this time, we can see how it would have been important to know who was a member of the race, and who was in fact a racial outsider. This preoccupation did not just concern the state. It was also of great concern to the ideological antisemites, committed to the supremacy of racial ideas. Antisemitic movements thrived because they painted a portrait of society in which the invisible Jew had a finger in every pie. He was diluting the race with disease and miscegenation, and threatening the nation with internationalist ideas of both the capitalist and the Marxist types. The only way to save the purity of the race and the success of the nation was to weed out the Jews!

It was this logic that eventually led to the popularity and feasibility of Nazi-style antisemitism. The systematic putting to death of Jews and other "undesirables" – the so-called Final Solution – was made possible because antisemitism and racism had been entirely rationalized within the logic of the Nazi regime. To go from mistrust, fear, and even hatred of the Jews to systematically rounding them up, herding them onto cattle trucks, and exporting them to their deaths on an industrial scale was only possible because the need to expunge the Jews from society became the primary prerequisite for the survival of the "Aryan race" from extinction. Dissent from this official belief was rare because, once allied to power and institutionalized in the laws and functions of the state, racism and antisemitism become both logical and self-perpetuating. The idea that it is necessary to kill one's enemy, once seen as an exception to the rule rather than a facet of the everyday business of governance, now became the rule. The growing banalization of modern social antisemitism that occurred in the years following 1880 in Europe is what enabled this highly significant change in perception.

The new judeophobia?

Unlike the years that led up to the Holocaust in Europe, antisemitism has not generally made regular headline news in recent decades. Overtly antisemitic ideas are mainly confined to the fringes of society, espoused only by extreme right-wing groups and admirers of Hitler. A vociferous but minority group of so-called Holocaust revisionist historians such as David Irving, Robert Faurisson, or Ernst Zundel continue to claim that the gas chambers did not exist and that the Holocaust was a hoax.

However, their work has been outlawed in many countries, they have served prison sentences, and some, such as David Irving, are even barred from entering certain countries.

Because of the atrocity of the Holocaust, antisemitism is publicly unacceptable. Nonetheless, the willingness to accept the widespread nature of antisemitism in the years leading to the Holocaust has not been as forthcoming. For example, it was not until 1995 that France officially admitted its role in the deportation of Jews during the Holocaust. However, such public admittance of guilt does not mean that the extent to which antisemitism shaped societal attitudes in the late nineteenth and twentieth centuries has been profoundly dealt with in Europe. Rather, like racism in general, antisemitism has most commonly been treated as a foreign importation, and most commonly, a German one. Other Europeans generally regard themselves, at worst, as passive bystanders who did not do enough to halt the atrocities, and at best, as coerced into obeying Nazi orders or risk deportation to the camps and death themselves.

While antisemitism today cannot be said to affect Jews in the West in the same way that racism against other minorities does on a daily basis, it has become an area of murky taboos mired in ill-defined and not fully understood senses of guilt. In recent years, in contrast, antisemitism has been the subject of rekindled discussion. Rather than being centered on the role of Jews within the societies in which they live, today's focus on antisemitism is connected to the actions of the State of Israel. Whereas the debate on the impact of Israeli Zionism on the Middle East has never been far from the agenda since Israel's occupation of the Palestinian territories in 1967 and the beginning of Palestinian armed resistance, it has taken on a particular significance since September 11, 2001. Since 1967, there has been an increase in international criticism of the Jewish state. Israel's disenfranchisement of the Palestinians and its colonization of their land has led many to oppose openly the ideology of Zionism, the movement that instigated the founding of a nation for the Jewish people in Palestine. The debate over anti-Zionism is a complicated one, yet it is important to dwell briefly on it because it brings the picture of modern antisemitism up to date.

The Middle East conflict between Israel and the Palestinians has attracted enormous – some would say disproportionate – interest around the globe. A variety of factions have a stake in the debate, including hardliners, radicals, and moderates on both sides. For those at one extreme of the debate, Zionism is equated with racism. For those at the other, anti-Zionism is antisemitism under a different guise. It is possible to argue that ideological Zionism has many strands, not all of which condone the occupation of Palestinian lands. Indeed, many proclaimed Zionists advocate a two-state solution to the Israeli–Palestinian conflict. However, it can also be said that the direction taken by the State of Israel in the name of its Zionist ideology has led to the racist discrimination of the Palestinian people, forced to live under occupation in their own country or as exiled refugees across the region and beyond.

The equation of Zionism with racism is at the nub of the contemporary debate about antisemitism. Those who defend the actions of the State of Israel condemn their critics as antisemitic. The logic is simple: Israel is a Jewish state. Therefore to criticize Israel one must be anti-Jewish. Jews who criticize Israel are "self-hating" Jews. Analysts of the problem point out that there is a lot at stake. In an era of terrorist threats identified as coming from a volatile Middle East and an oil-dependent global economy that is put at risk by any tipping of the balance of power between the West and the Arab nations that control much of the world's oil output, the problem is clearly a political one. The fate of a tiny country such as Israel–Palestine and both of its peoples raises so much interest because of its interconnection with much bigger stakes.

Against this backdrop, noting of the rise in antisemitism in recent years has always been linked to the attitudes of those who are said to be the enemies of Israel, and by association, of Jews in general. A country where antisemitism has registered a rise since the mid-1990s with a surge in attacks, mainly on Jewish monuments and cemeteries, is France. In *The New Judeophobia*, Pierre-André Taguieff argues that anti-Jewish sentiment is rife in France. He claims that the rise in violation of Jewish places of worship and other sites is proof that there is a "new Judeophobia" that "never before in the France of the post-war . . . has circulated in as many social milieus, meeting as little intellectual and political resistance" (2002: 11).

The group Taguieff singles out as the main instigator of antisemitism today is Muslim youth. They are part of a global trend of young people of Muslim origin who identify with the Palestinian, and now also the Iraqi, struggle as symbolic of their own condition of exclusion in their societies. However, recognizing the anger that many of these young people (and many other non-Muslims including Jews) feel against Israel, is different from blaming all young Muslims, as a group, for the rise in antisemitic attacks. Such generalized stereotyping ironically mirrors the antisemitic identification of all Jews with the actions of a few unscrupulous bankers a century ago.

Unlike the antisemitic movements of the nineteenth and early twentieth centuries, today's level of antisemitism is not at epidemic levels, although there are differences across countries, with Eastern European societies in particular still harboring a marked antisemitism. Despite this, an understandable anxiety lingers from the long years of Jewish persecution. There is a feeling among many Jews that another genocide is possible, given the right conditions. However, according to those who critique the idea of a "new Judeophobia," this feeling is based on a failure to understand the historic parallels between the antisemitism suffered by Jews in the past and the racism that affects other minority groups today. While there are certainly some who cling mercilessly to antisemitic beliefs, and a minority who will even act on them, the focus of hatred has shifted to other groups, stigmatized as the Jews once were.

For many Jews, on the contrary, it is these other minority groups, in particular those they associate with an antisemitic Islamic agenda, that are responsible for the new wave of antisemitism. This fails to account for the fact that ideological racism in general has most commonly been instigated by elites. The history of modern antisemitic movements, founded mainly by right-wing nationalists, aristocrats, and Church leaders, attests to this. This insight is lost in the powerful combination of feelings based on a lingering fear of persecution, the belief that the existence of Israel is necessary as a safe haven for Jews who may again have to flee at any moment, and an anger against those who dare make comparisons between the treatment of the Palestinians and other oppressed peoples today and the Jews of yesterday. While many Jews resist these feelings and opt to add their voices to those who criticize all forms of racism, there are many who cling to the idea of the Jews as that most hated of outsiders.

The powerful emotive nature of the debate on anti-Zionism and antisemitism is complicated by the involvement of contemporary politics. In the United States, Israel's foremost ally, it is of prime importance which side of the debate public figures such as politicians and academics stand on. It can determine their success or failure in public life. In recent years, organizations such as Campus Watch have been established to "monitor" academics who espouse views that are critical of Israel. Outspoken opponents of Israel, including Jews, have been personally attacked for their views. In 2007, Norman Finkelstein, author of *The Holocaust Industry*, a book that examines what the author calls "the exploitation of Jewish suffering" for the purposes of the Zionist agenda, was refused tenure at his university following a campaign against him, ultimately leading him to resign from his post at De Paul University.

The veteran Israeli peace campaigner, Uri Avnery, describes the situation as a paradox. Israel has itself created contemporary antisemitism: by branding all of its critics antisemites, it has revived antisemitism because it is not possible, according to Israel and its defenders, to criticize Israel and not be antisemitic. Because of the old fear of antisemitism and the belief that the existence of a Jewish homeland provides a safe haven for Jews, Jewish communities around the world are forced to defend the actions of Israel. This creates a vicious circle, according to Avnery. Because Jews defend Israel, they soon become identified with its actions, leading indeed to the creation of antisemitism. Avnery (2003: 46) calls for Jews to "break out of the vicious circle. Disarm the anti-Semites . . . Let your conscience speak out." Only this will halt what could be the return of antisemitism when all Jews are unjustifiably connected to the actions of a government that claims to act in their name.

The strange career of antisemitism, from the 1880s to the present day, and its confusion with the not uncontestable but wholly different position of anti-Zionism, holds important lessons for the discussion of racism in general. In particular, if we are motivated by a desire to challenge racism and hope that it will one day be overcome, the debate on the "new Judeophobia" raises serious concerns. Those who equate the return of antisemitism with protest against the treatment of Palestinians contribute to destroying the possibility of creating strong alliances against racism, antisemitism, and Islamophobia. The contemporary paranoia, prejudice, and ostracism against Muslims in Western societies mirrors the treatment of the Jews in pre-war Europe. While hindsight has shown us that illogical arguments were used to condone antisemitism in the past, we find it difficult to accept that the curtailing of the civil liberties of Muslims today is based on blanket stereotyping of the Muslim community that connects all its members to the actions of an extreme minority. Fears about Muslim "extremists" today mirrors those about Jewish Bolsheviks and anarchists, migrants from Eastern Europe to the US and Europe, at the turn of the twentieth century. Although racism takes different forms in various places and times and in the way it is manifested against different groups of people, it is repetitive in terms of the effects it has on the lives of people. The lessons of modern anti-semitism are perhaps more pertinent now than at any time since the liberation of Auschwitz.

Racism without race?

Andrew Sullivan has a post on how Barak Obama is allegedly a candidate for post-racial America. If I may be so bold, let me suggest that a post-racial country would not be obsessing over a presidential candidate's alleged post-racialness. America is not so much post-racial as getting-over-the-subject-but-not-quite-there-racial.

Chris Hallquist (February 18, 2007)
http://uncrediblehallq.blogspot.com

Racism has become bound up, in myriad complex ways, with how the modern nation-state works. It has entered into culture and determined social interaction, thus having a direct effect on individuals' lives. The idea of race that underpins racism maintains white privilege and continues to influence the way in which those we think of as "minorities" experience life in Western societies. Racism can be outspoken and aggressive – leading to death and genocide – or tacit and institutionalized – resulting in the often unseen and varied discrimination against whole sectors of our societies. Despite this, it is increasingly argued that racism is a thing of the past. This is linked to a second, and rather different argument, that we are, or should be, living in a post-racial age. This chapter examines these views.

The idea that racism is a thing of the past originates in a variety of quarters that often differ significantly from each other. There are those who argue that racism is quite simply unimportant, a figment of its victims' imagination. This line of thought tends to mask what is in fact a racist argument; one that refuses to admit that injustice against racialized others exists at all. It is very similar to the arguments of Holocaust deniers who negate the existence of the gas chambers but who claim (sometimes in secret) that they would have been a good idea.

A second line of reasoning sees racism as an episode in history that is now over. This is divided into two different ways of seeing things. The first simply sees racism as belonging to chapters in history that are officially closed. For example, the end of racial segregation kept in place by the Jim Crow "separate but equal" laws in the United States in 1965, or the collapse of the apartheid regime in South Africa in 1994, were seen by many to mark the end of racism. This view, although correctly seeing racism as historical and contextual, fails to see how official refutations of racism are not enough to eradicate it. Not only do racist sentiments linger among those in the American Deep South or the Afrikaner community, racism is still institutionalized in both the United States and South Africa despite having been outlawed by the system. The cultural and political changes that have to be undergone for racism to disappear are still to come in most places, particularly where they have been so deeply embedded.

Those who see racism as a thing of the past may also see the Holocaust as an aberration. According to this view, the Nazi death camps have something particular to tell us about the German psyche. Taken to an extreme, this means continuing to treat even those Germans born years after the end of Nazism with suspicion. This rather common view rules out the contrary one, laid out in the previous chapter, that sees Auschwitz as historically contingent and as a possible outcome of the modern condition, arising from the exclusionary nature of the nation-state. This view naturalizes racism as if it were a personality trait of certain groups of people, or of certain nations. It is an ahistorical view that is not borne out by the fact that racism has taken root in so many societies. The fact that racism manifests itself in often very different ways from place to place should not lead us to be comforted by the notion that it is the preserve of some countries and not of others. Racism has been a predominant feature of most, if not all, Western societies.

A second, but interlinked, argument is the main theme of this chapter. This is the view that we are living in a post-racial age. Although as we shall see, this notion at times overlaps with the idea that racism is a thing of the past, it is an intellectually more developed view that, therefore, needs to be considered in detail. Taken at face value, the idea that we live in a post-racial age seems to echo the idea that racism is a thing of the past, relegated to particular moments of history. On closer examination, however, the argument is slightly different. It admits that racism is still a feature of our lives today, but argues that the term "racism" is misleading because the idea that races exist has been proven wrong. "Racism" is actually a bad term because it is based on a false premise, namely that there is something called a race. If we agree that races do not objectively exist and that science has proven that all human beings belong to the same species – the human race – which is not subdivisible, then surely we cannot speak of racism!

On paper at least, this argument makes perfect sense. However, this position has led to the argument that because it is meaningless to speak about race we also have to question whether *racism* actually continues to exist. Taken to extremes, this point of view has led to a failure to take racism seriously or even to its complete denial, and has underpinned moves away from the commitment to redress racial inequality.

Refusing to see race

> Racelessness is the neoliberal attempt to go beyond – without (fully) coming to terms with – racial histories and their accompanying racist inequities and iniquities. (Goldberg 2002: 221)

Racism has often been pushed to the sidelines as a subject of serious inquiry. This has mainly been done either by insisting that racism is an age-old phenomenon, a mere fact of human nature, unavoidable, and as such not to be taken too seriously. Alternatively, racism has been seen as linked only to the false idea that humanity is divided into races: once we debunk that idea, racism becomes a thing of the past. Unfortunately, neither of these two claims holds water from a historical point of view. This is because they both fail to see how race and racism are invested in politics. In other words, racism does not stand alone; it is bound up with the way our societies function. "Racelessness" is a shorthand for this failure to admit the persistent impact of race. The argument for seeing race is not based on a wish to revive race as biology, but on the recognition that the effects of racial division continue to have a profound impact on society and politics.

The debate over whether or not we should continue to refer to race in writing about racism has obscured much of what is important about the debate. While in Europe since the end of the Second World War, race has become almost unmentionable, in the United States in particular the word race continues to be used as purely descriptive. We are all familiar with the descriptions of crime suspects in popular US television shows – "Caucasian male, brown hair, average height." The use of the racial descriptor "Caucasian," which has outlasted references to "Negro," now replaced by black or African-American, is rarely put into question. It is commonplace for people to refer colloquially to "my" race and for

THE UNESCO TRADITION

In 1950, UNESCO issued a "Statement against Race and Racial Prejudice" drawn up by social and natural scientists. The spirit of the Statement continues to dominate the approach to racism of most Western governments today. The UNESCO Tradition is based on two central premises. First, it was proposed that racism had to be tackled on its own grounds. The panel of UNESCO experts believed that racism was a pseudo-science rather than a political idea. Therefore, to defeat racism, it was sufficient to disprove the theory of race from a scientific point of view. Once this was achieved, it was believed that racism would no longer hold water. Secondly, the UNESCO approach was based on the related idea that, despite the fact that races do not exist, differences between human beings do, and need to be explained, especially in the face of a growing immigrant population. Motivated by the work of anthropologists working in so-called "primitive" societies, UNESCO explained the differences between human beings in terms of ethnicity. As Lévi-Strauss claimed, while races do not exist, cultural differences between human beings do, and these variations are due to ethnicity, which explains the human propensity to live in tribe-like groups. However, the belief was that by replacing race with ethnicity and racism with ethnocentrism, which was seen as a more explanatory term, the problems of racism would disappear. This belief did not take account of the fact that it was not whether we call it race or ethnicity, racism or ethnocentrism, that is important. Rather, if we do not challenge the assumptions that lie behind dividing people into different groups and essentializing their identities, the problem that we call racism will fail to go away.

administrative forms to ask for one's race to be identified. Paul Gilroy, in *Against Race*, argues that the fact that the word "race" is used so unproblematically means that it should now be rejected. He claims that using race in this way proves that the discussion of race and racism has been completely depoliticized. For Gilroy, the emphatic reference to race used to have political meaning as an act of reclamation, much like the use of "queer" by gay activists. However, in today's world, which he sees as more cosmopolitan and diverse, he believes the moment for political statements of this kind is over. His argument, insomuch as it refers to tackling racism, is an important one. But he may be seen as focusing too much on semantics in a way that does not really get over the fact that racism appears to be here to stay.

The avoidance of the word "race" has sometimes been linked to the refusal to recognize racism. Goldberg discusses the concept of racelessness in his book *The Racial State*. His argument, which uses examples from the United States, South Africa, Brazil, and Europe, is that racelessness sums up the way racism works today. He traces the origins of racelessness to racial historicism that, as discussed in Chapter 1, came to dominance in the nineteenth and twentieth centuries, coexisting with and gradually taking over from the more overt naturalist racism. Racelessness became central to historicist ideas, over time becoming the primary expression of racism. Racelessness, therefore, is far from being non-*racist*.

Naturalism and historicism are distinguished from each other because, while naturalism insists on the importance of race, historicism does the opposite. In the bid to "civilize the natives," historicists set out precisely *not* to see their race. But this not seeing, Goldberg claims, is the crux of the matter. It allows for racism too to go unseen. Over time, the conscious undertaking to erase race became the dominant mode of historicist thinking. However, this erasure was only concerned with race as it marked out those who were different from the dominant group in Western societies: whites. The decision not to see race meant at the same time that it was possible for whiteness, now seen as having nothing to do with race, to become the norm or standard. Racelessness is in fact synonymous with whiteness. Although the promise of racelessness in democratic societies is that everyone, regardless of the color of their skin, their ethnic origin, or religion, will be treated the same, in reality it is necessary to conform to a mode of being that is ultimately unattainable. It is impossible for those who are not white to attain the standard of whiteness, not only because their skin color bars them from doing so, but because whiteness comes with a code of behaviors and ways of doing things that are seen as being only knowable by whites.

We can seen this notion at work in claims that ethnic minorities "know no better" because their traditions influence them to act in a way that is contrary to the way things are done "over here." This patronizing claim is based on the idea that, first, there is a way of doing things that is instantly knowable to "us" and intangible to "them" and, second, that despite our best efforts, the cultural traditions of "minorities" will always be more important to them than those of the "host community." This idea underlies the more politically correct formulations of the anti-immigration stance. But it is particularly flagrant when used in reference to minorities born and brought up in Western societies, often with little or no connection to their grandparents' places of origin.

The significance of racelessness is in the fact that it allows for this type of separation and inequality between whites and "others" to go unhindered because it has been completely dislocated from the ugliness of race. The triumph of historicism means that we commonly accept the idea that racism is only of the easily identified naturalist kind. According to this view, "real" racism is based on dangerous, pseudo-scientific theories, and results in genocide. Under this schema, racism of the historicist variety described by Goldberg does not exist. Racism can therefore be portrayed as a closed chapter of history. In the aftermath of the Second World War and in the era of decolonization, historicist racism could continue because its main premise – racelessness – was seen as being the very antithesis of racism. It is therefore easy to understand why many ask why *would* it be racist to refuse to see race as significant? This, above all, is the success of racelessness.

Racelessness, according to Goldberg, has taken many forms in different places since the mid-twentieth century. He claims that the principle of non-racialism in South Africa, racial democracy in Brazil, and ethnic pluralism and multiculturalism in Canada, Australia, and Europe are all examples of the way the principle of racelessness has permitted racial historicism to persist. All these systems and policies formally treat everyone as if they were alike. This may seem to be a desirable principle. However, if we unpick it, treating everyone as if they were alike is not the same as ensuring equality. To ensure equality, it is necessary to factor in the injustices suffered by some and the privileges enjoyed by others and to redress the balance. The failure to do so is at the heart of the problem of colorblindness.

US legal scholar Patricia Williams begins her book, *Seeing a Colorblind Future*, with an anecdote about her son. In his nursery school, the teachers suspected that the little boy was colorblind. She sent him for tests, but his vision was normal. In fact, her son was saying, not that he did not *know* which color was which, but that it was not *important* whether the grass was green or the sky was blue. Well-meaning teachers had put so much effort into ensuring that their pupils understood that it did not matter what color a person's skin was that Williams's child took them literally: color simply does not matter.

Williams uses this anecdote to demonstrate how colorblind policies in the United States have got the wrong end of the stick. She says that colorblindness in practice does not mean treating everyone equally. Rather it means pretending that the fact that people are different does not matter, just as her son believed that whether grass is purple or green is immaterial. She compares this state of affairs to the three monkeys, Hear No Evil, See No Evil, Speak No Evil. If we do not mention the fact that someone is different then maybe her difference will go away. As underlined in Chapter 2, difference in modern Western societies has been racialized. Therefore, when we speak of difference, buried within there is a reference to race. This is because the legacy of race is the tendency to naturalize difference, to see it as fundamentally, inextricably, and inherently different, and so not open to change. This is why we cannot skip over race as if it belonged to a bygone era and move unchallenged into the colorblind age. The legacy of race itself is crucial to the need to frame matters from the perspective of colorblindness in the first place. Why is this so?

Goldberg claims that colorblindness is the best way of ensuring that white privilege can continue in multi-ethnic societies. Colorblindness can be seen as what he calls crisis management, a way of not letting the new-found freedoms of the post-civil rights, post-decolonization era get out of control. The best way of maintaining this control is to insist on the supremacy of Western, democratic (white) law as the best possible means of ensuring equality. In simpler terms, the historicist logic that the West embodies progress was taken to mean that non-whites, immigrants, and decolonized nations could rely on the Western system to show them the way.

Colorblindness, therefore, is not applied universally. Because whiteness is not seen as a color, being blind to color literally means being "blind to *people* of color" (Goldberg 2002: 223). The consequence of this is two-fold. Firstly, being colorblind brings about an artificial way of relating to the diverse make-up of the majority of Western urbanized societies today. Because racelessness is equated with whiteness, colorblindness in practice means seeing everyone as white. However, we know this is not the case. This leaves us with the predicament of not knowing how to talk about difference. A lot of the frustration expressed about "political correctness" is part of the misplaced outcome of this inability to discuss difference. We have been told that it is wrong, rude even, to remark on another's difference. Yet we can see that people *do* differ and cannot understand why there is something wrong about pointing out that simple fact. Although, to be sure, a lot of what passes for "pointing out simple facts" is an excuse for racism, this is an understandable frustration. The result of enforcing a principle of colorblindness is, paradoxically, that those of color, and the racialized in general (for this is not confined to skin color) begin to stick out like sore thumbs! The presence of those who look and act differently among us is not experienced comfortably. It is all the more noticeable because we are told we should not point it out.

The second effect of colorblindness is in its impact on policy. This has been particularly significant in the United States, as demonstrated by the revocation of the principle of affirmative action. Affirmative action policies, first advocated by John F. Kennedy in the midst of the battle for civil rights in the 1960s, create opportunities for people from disadvantaged backgrounds to access jobs and educational possibilities from which they were previously excluded. Since the heyday of the civil rights movement, conservative forces in the United States have outspokenly criticized affirmative action. Since the 1990s, campaigners such as the African-American Republican Ward Connerly and his American Civil Rights Institute, have put affirmative action policies into question, especially in US academic institutions where they had been most widely applied.

As Williams points out, the move to revoke affirmative action policies in US higher education admissions policy is paradoxical because it sets out to remove all reference to race while trying to remedy the problem of racism. The removal of affirmative action is based on two arguments: First, that it favors groups on the basis of their ethnic origin alone, rather than on the merit of each individual. This view is summarized by a comment on the US Web site CampusProgress.org:

> Like the union movement, affirmative action has outlived its usefulness in this society . . . The problem with those who fight for affirmative action is that they don't see that they are telling minorities that they are not capable of competing on their own and that they can't make it without the assistance of others. People are most successful when they pull themselves up by their own bootstraps and decide on their own what it is that they want to do with their lives. (http://www.campusprogress. org/tools/230/)

This argument cannot account for the failure in reality to apply the principles of meritocracy universally. Neither can it respond to the fact that in the US, because of racism past and present, there are certain groups whose merit will never be judged unless they are given a chance to prove themselves through affirmative action programs. Following the 1998 banning of the use of state funds for affirmative action policies to support minority students or faculty members at the University of California (Proposition 209), the numbers of black students and faculty have decreased dramatically. As Goldberg points out, out of eight hundred engineering students admitted to the University of California at Berkeley in 2005, not a single one was African-American. The argument made by those who support affirmative action is that unless conscious, radical, and sometimes unpopular moves are made to redress racism, the status quo will reign.

The second argument against affirmative action is that it is actually racism in reverse. In the United States, the idea that affirmative action reduces possibilities for whites, leading to their marginalization, is promoted by the highly publicized cases of a handful of white students who have "lost out" because of quotas reserved for minorities. An example of such a case is that of Jennifer Gratz who now campaigns full-time against affirmative action. Gratz failed to be admitted to the University of Michigan in 1995. Her court case against the university led to the points system it used to rank applicants, with students from minority and disadvantaged backgrounds being awarded an extra 20 points out of a total 150, being made illegal (although the university's affirmative action policy was not completely overturned). She argued that she had been racially discriminated against because she is white. Although white students with outstanding grades could not be overlooked in favor of less highly achieving minority students, Gratz's average grades meant that she was passed over for a student whom the university considered to be more deserving. As the *Boston Globe* reported in 2007, contrary to popular belief that cases like Gratz's are widespread, Michigan's policy prior to the ruling against it was far from being the norm. Universities in the US consistently admit white students with less than exemplary grades because their families can afford to support the universities financially. Applying to up to fifteen percent of freshman enrollments, such cases lead to discrimination against blacks *and* whites whose parents cannot pay their children's way into an elite college. Nevertheless, the belief that affirmative action is barring the way for whites in education and employment is strongly promoted.

The ideas of racelessness, of a post-racial order, and of reverse racism belong to a logic that Goldberg has called "racial Americanization." This is based on his view that racism takes different forms in different places around the world. However, the hegemony of the US in contemporary global politics means that this brand of racism is gaining ground beyond the borders of the USA. The history of today's racial Americanization goes back to the civil rights era of the 1960s. This time of struggle constituted a break with classic US racism, based on a bloody history of colonial domination, slavery, segregation, and often murder. Although black people in the USA were traditionally predominantly rural, their migration to the cities during the first decades of the twentieth century meant that, by 1950, the majority of black people were urban dwellers. To a higher degree than any other ethnic minority group in the USA, by 1940 ninety-three percent of black people in cities lived in majority black areas. The struggle of the civil rights movement focused heavily on the effects of segregation. As Goldberg shows, despite the fact that since the 1940s, US government policy had been leading towards desegregation, at the same time private interests in the country were re-entrenching segregation both within individual cities and across them, leading to the emergence of fourteen majority black cities across the

USA, despite the fact that, today, African-Americans make up only thirteen percent of the population.

Re-segregation, it is argued, is due to personal preference, with members of all ethno-racial groups, so it is said, preferring to live "among their own." However, as Goldberg points out, white people claim to prefer to live in neighborhoods where eighty percent of the population is white, but when questioned, black people said they preferred to live in neighborhoods with a fifty percent white population, hence showing a preference for diversity. The consequence is that what is painted as personal preference is generated by the dominant culture in which (1) blacks are seen as undesirable neighbors, and (2) living among one's own ethnic or racial group is considered more "natural." Far from being natural, these beliefs are generated by an "activist segregationism" (Goldberg 2006a: 83) promoted in politics, economics, law, and culture with the specific aim of ensuring that national desegregation policies were doomed from the start.

As Goldberg explains, re-segregation is ensured by the privatization of all common resources from roads to healthcare and schools. Because being racialized in the United States is often linked to being poor, the effect of privatization is that only those who can afford to pay for toll roads, good schools, and private healthcare will live in the areas where these are provided. These services only exist in the areas where the residents can afford to pay for them. Because, under the present climate, the US government supports the conservative logic that poverty, crime, unemployment, etc., are the result of personal failure, areas where the predominantly poor and racialized live are inadequately serviced by the state. In other words, if it cannot be paid for, a decent school, hospital, or road will simply not exist. Under this rubric, it is easy to see how segregation continues to define much of US society. The US Center on Budget and Policy Priorities reported in 2006 that between one-quarter and one-third of black and Latino families live in hardship, as opposed to fourteen percent of white families. Whites, therefore, find it easier to ensure that their families are brought up in areas where they can access a reasonable standard of living.

Living comfortably is directly aligned to living in white-only zones. This means that people of different ethno-racial groups simply do not know each other, because as children they are brought up separately and look forward to very different futures. Under these conditions, it is inevitable that all groups in US society have preconceived stereotypes about each other, borne of their ignorance of one another's ways of life. But this is not equal because it is white lifestyles that are held up as the norm, reinforced by the media. Therefore, anyone failing to live by what is considered to be the normal standards set by white society is considered a failure. This personalized vision of the world fails to take power and domination into account as factors that effect both racism and classism. Indeed, neither are considered to exist objectively beyond the minds of poor people and minorities mired in the "victim culture."

"Breaking the levees"

What we saw unfold in the days after the hurricane was the most naked manifestation of conservative social policy towards the poor, where the message for decades has been: "You are on your own." (Cornel West, 2005)

In 2005, Hurricane Katrina ripped through New Orleans, a city with a sixty-seven percent black population, engulfing the city in water. The fact that the city was inadequately protected against flooding was due to the segregated living arrangements of blacks and whites. White people mainly lived in gated communities on the hills overlooking the bay, while blacks populated the downtown areas. Their location and their access to private means of transport allowed the majority of whites to flee the flooded city. By contrast, most blacks, who did not have the means to escape (public transportation was not ensured) were left either to drown or to see their homes destroyed, leaving them with nothing. In New Orleans up to fifty percent of black people lived in poverty, double the national average. Left homeless, black citizens were rounded up by the army and herded into the Superdome or the Convention Center, in what have been described as "prison-like conditions" (Goldberg 2006b: 90).

When the rapper Kanye West claimed that "President Bush doesn't care about black people" he was referring not only to the neglectful policies that led the levees to break or to the fact that New Orleans blacks have always, as Cornel West claims, lived in the "Third World," he was also thinking about the state's response to Katrina during which the people who were made refugees in their own city became the targets of the army's aggressive moves to maintain social order. Countless news stories described black people turned looters who were reported to be ransacking stores in the hurricane's aftermath. As MSNBC reported on August 30, 2005:

> At a Walgreen's drugstore in the French Quarter, people were running out with grocery baskets and coolers full of soft drinks, chips and diapers. When police finally showed up, a young boy stood in the door screaming, "86! 86!" – the radio code for police – and the crowd scattered. (http://www.msnbc.msn.com/id/9131493)

Little was said about the fact that the food, drink, and diapers being stolen were not luxury items, but necessities that were not provided at the "shelters" housing the homeless. A tourist who witnessed the looting exclaimed: "It's downtown Baghdad . . . It's insane. I've wanted to come here for ten years. I thought this was a sophisticated city. I guess not." To Goldberg, this is not far from the truth. The National Guard in New Orleans was reinforced by employees from companies such as Blackhawk Security recently returned from Iraq. They were left to fire freely on presumed looters. "New Orleans was, in a nutshell, simply Iraq come home" (Goldberg 2006b: 90).

The consequence of Hurricane Katrina is that New Orleans will no longer be a majority black city. Few black people will be able to afford to live there, according to the plans of the US Department of Housing and Urban Development. They will be dispersed to other cities where their presence will be less noticed than it was in pre-Katrina New Orleans. And because the link to racism and the privatization of segregation is rarely made in mainstream US commentary, the whitening of New Orleans will not be seen in the context of race. The success of the discourse of racelessness and post-racism has been to disconnect issues such as housing, employment, wages, education, healthcare, life expectancy, and transport from racism. Poverty is seen as due to bad personal management or as ethno-racially inherent, never the result of racial domination.

What are the effects of racelessness and ideas such as colorblindness on our relationship to race and racism today? For Goldberg, the triumph of racelessness has led to an ahistorical acceptance of race. In other words, categories such as white and black, Asian or Oriental are seen as being just ways of describing people, as good as any other. Racelessness has managed to erase from political memory the fact that these are racial terms and that we would not give the same meaning to whiteness or blackness were it not for the pernicious history of racism. We therefore skim over the specifics of racism: the murderous histories of slavery and colonialism barely get a mention in many school textbooks.

Moreover, racelessness has reduced everything to the same level. There is no sense that racism is something specific that is located in the processes of racialization and the histories of racial science, colonial domination, slavery, genocide, etc. On the contrary, racism becomes a catch-all phrase that can be used to describe almost any situation. It is used to refer to any situation of discrimination or unfairness. By the same logic, we hear talk of "reverse racism." Affirmative action is repackaged as racism against whites, or the anti-colonial movement put on a par with the Ku Klux Klan. In the current debate about immigration in Australia, the idea that white people are the victims of an onslaught against their lifestyle and culture at the hands of foreign migrants is a constant theme.

Finally, racelessness strips the state of responsibility for the continuing situation of racial inequality. It does so by making individuals entirely responsible for their own situation. Because policies such as colorblindness officially hold out the opportunity for everyone to achieve in a supposed racial meritocracy, those who do not do so only have themselves to blame. Ethnic minorities and people of color are portrayed as making use of their origins in order to climb the career ladder. This notion is of course unfounded in the face of the discrimination in employment, education, and other spheres that exists for a majority of minority ethnic groups. In the context of racelessness, however, victory is reserved for those who are perceived to succeed in life without having to mention race.

The problem of wishing for a world without race is not that it is not desirable, but that it is not yet possible. One of the most important thinkers on race and racism, the African-American W.E.B. Du Bois, explained that race is not important in itself. What is important is what he called the *badge* of race rather than race itself. Du Bois's badge of race refers not to biology, but to the "physical bond" that the "common history" of those who "have suffered a long disaster and have one long memory" have to carry with them (Du Bois 1940, cited in Appiah 1985: 33). In other words, we cannot forget race because it stands for the injustices of the past and the present; injustices that have very often not been admitted and that, furthermore, are erased by the declaration that we are living in a raceless world where colorblindness ensures equal treatment. As Du Bois predicted, little could be further from the truth.

The return of biology?

As we have seen, the idea that we are living in a post-racial age is belied by the fact that discrimination based on perceived racial differences between groups of ethno-racially defined people remains a factor in many of our societies. The arguments against racelessness or color-blindness work with the assumption that while race is socially constructed, racism continues to affect the lives of many people around the world. However, the conservative denial of the significance of the discriminatory effects of race go hand-in-hand with an acceptance of the salience of race as a determinant of the differences between human beings. In sum, despite the condemnations of the explanatory capacity of race going back sixty years, politicians, scientists, and other influential public figures in many Western countries continue to believe in and instrumentalize racial difference.

This does not mean, however, that there is a return to the racial science of the "Golden Age" of racism. The link between race and science being made today is more subtle. Two main points should be considered. First, the "return" of biological racism is linked to the idea that there is a new racism. The new racism was first noted in the 1980s. It is closely linked to ideas about racelessness. Rather than resorting to old pseudo-scientific theories about biological differences, the new racism focuses on cultural incompatibility as the main reason why segregation or strict immigration policies should be enforced. However, as Martin Barker noted in 1981, these cultural differences are naturalized in the same way as the old biologically defined racial hierarchies. When we hear arguments expressed by politicians, in the media, or by ordinary people that people of different cultures are "better off" in their own countries or neighborhoods, not because they are inferior but because they are different, this post-racial argument is racism in thin disguise. Second, there are those who propose that race continues to have scientific meaning that can lend insight into many spheres. They counter the claim that using race scientifically infers a racial hierarchy. However, these ideas are a prominent part of the human genome diversity project that some critics have claimed cannot be seen as entirely free of racist bias. The continued significance of biological notions of race are important because they frame many of the policies examined in the previous section that, although portrayed as race-neutral, are actually underpinned by a strongly racialized worldview.

Analyses of the new racism generally assume that, in making the new racist argument, culture completely supersedes biology. In contrast, Martin Barker closely links culture and biology. The new racism is a theory of "pseudo-biological culturalism" (Barker 1981: 23). As explained in detail in Chapter 2, to understand racism we must understand how its main function is the naturalization and essentializing of human characteristics. These can be biological: skin color, supposed mental abilities, sexuality, etc. But they can also be cultural: the tendency to behave in a certain way or live according to particular moral codes. Not only does the new racism observed by Barker mirror racialization – we could call the process "culturalization," it bases itself upon what is proposed as a scientific theory. The idea that people belonging to different cultural groups should live together, each in their own "natural" home – the argument used against immigration or desegregation – is portrayed as being instinctive. This is because, it is said, we are genetically programmed to have these preferences. The new racism thesis proposes that,

> it is in our biology, our instincts, to defend our way of life, traditions and customs against outsiders. This is a non-rational process; and none the worse for it. For we are soaked in, made up out of, our traditions and our culture. (Barker 1981: 23–4)

The beauty of this idea is that those who propose it can avoid being accused of racism because it is based on the argument that *all* human groups share the instinct to want to live separately from others.

Barker notes a cross-fertilization between the emergence of new racist ideas in 1980s Britain and parallel ideas being developed in the natural sciences that supported it. Two interrelated disciplines in particular, based on zoology and biology, made a remarkable contribution: ethology and sociobiology.

The discipline of ethology can be defined as the science of the formation of national and collective, as well as individual, character. It was made highly popular by the books and television series of one of its principle advocates, Desmond Morris. Sociobiology is the application of evolutionary theory to social behavior. It is represented by figures such as Richard Dawkins, author of the highly popular book, *The Selfish Gene*. Both disciplines emerge from the Darwinist theory of evolution and, in particular, the theory of natural selection. Natural selection is the process by which organisms ensure their survival by prioritizing the lives of the fitter among them. Those with the characteristics best adapted to the environment in which they live survive, while the weaker die. The transfer of these fitter genes from generation to generation leads gradually to the transformation of the species as a whole.

The argument of ethologists and sociobiologists is not the same as that of the Social Darwinists or eugenicists who radically argued for putting weaker members of a race to death in order to strengthen the "race nation" as a whole. Coming from a different perspective, both disciplines claim that they can explain racism from a biological or genetic point of view. They thus claim to be non-racist and, moreover, to have found the answer to the question of why racism exists. However, according to Martin Barker, a closer look at what these scientists say reveals the opposite to be true. The ethologists' and sociobiologists' "explanation" of racism is racist in itself. How so?

The argument of those in both camps is slightly different. However, their political significance is the same and both have influenced the new racism thesis. Briefly, ethologists make two main points. First, Desmond Morris, for example, argues that it is incorrect to see the stereotypical traits of different national groups (e.g. excitable Italians, laborious Germans, etc.) as innate. However, the *belief* we have that national characteristics are innate is natural and universal. Morris argues that all human groups are biologically more or less the same. Therefore one of the traits that all groups share is the tendency to form groups and to believe that each group is unique. To recap, it is not that perceived differences between human groups are either innate or significant. Rather, the belief that we all share that such differences are innate and that they are of primary importance is a fundamental part of human nature, according to the ethologists.

A second idea of the ethologists is said to explain why racism occurs. If all human groups agree that the tendency to live in unique communities is innate, then it is necessary to explain how these communities are preserved. Ethologists use the idea of "redirected aggression" to explain this. Aggression is fundamental to ethologists in their observation of animal behavior. Why do animals tend not to kill those from among their own species? Aggression has an important evolutionary function and therefore does not disappear as a result of natural selection, like many other useless or harmful traits. What happens is that this natural aggression is redirected onto those from outside the group. And this redirected aggression has a positive effect on the internal strength of one's own group. According to ethologists, we can only love those of our own group if we have adequately displaced our aggression. In fact, the stronger the group, the more aggression has been redirected. We do not do this consciously; it is instinctive. The problem with such ideas is obviously that ethologists like Morris have applied what is basically the observation of animal behavior not only to human beings, but to whole nations, or ethnic groups.

The arguments of the sociobiologists are less centered on aggression. Central to them is Dawkins's idea of the "selfish gene." This is the notion that ensuring the survival of one's own group is primordial; all other groups, therefore, are one's natural competitors. Sociobiology has been adapted to the explanation of human behavior more than ethology has. The work of Pierre van den Berghe, once a sociologist of race relations who became a proponent of sociobiology in the late 1970s, has been particularly influential. He explains that racism, nationalism, and ethnocentrism are all the result of what sociobiology calls "kin altruism," the inbuilt tendency to want to help and protect those of our own kin group. He believes that the growth in human beings' genetic strength over time led to the tendency to organize in ever larger groups. For the creation of nations to be successful, it became increasingly important to be able to fight against other groups and protect ethnic boundaries. Altruism within one's group, therefore, goes hand-in-hand with hostility towards outsiders. Racism, which according to the sociobiologists is part and parcel of kin altruism, is simply programmed in us genetically.

What both ethology and sociobiology offer us is a scientific means of explaining the commonsense feelings that motivate the new racism. Barker calls this instinctivism. Instinctivism, or the idea of protecting one's group against outsiders in the unstoppable interests of evolution, provides a neat justification of immigration policy. It also explains why racism is unavoidable and, more importantly, why it is universal. The argument goes that if Australians were to find themselves immigrants in, to take a well-known case, Afghanistan, they would expect to face the same treatment meted out to Afghan immigrants in Australia. It is simply what we are genetically programmed to do. It is not difficult to see why this argument would have so much appeal: ethologists and sociobiologists protect themselves from the charge of racism because they say they are merely contributing to explaining why racism persists. However, when allied to the political ambitions of certain political parties and lobby groups and used to justify policy, it is clear how these pseudo-scientific ideas are, when applied to humans, in fact motivated by racism.

What Barker flagged in the early 1980s was the beginning of an ever closer relationship between science and politics that is mediated, whether explicitly or implicitly, by race. He drew attention to the fact that governments, particularly in contentious areas such as immigration, crime, and security, rely increasingly on scientific explanations to legitimate their actions. The evolution of ideas in ethology and sociobiology is not dissociated from the preoccupation today with genetics, in particular DNA. These zoological/biological and genetic fields all claim to be able to tell us about the proneness of human groups to a range of diseases and behaviors. So far this seems unproblematic. However, research into human genetics as a means of studying our origins and of our likelihood, therefore, to develop certain dispositions is not unconnected to the idea that there are racial variations that differentiate between human beings.

Looking at the recent contribution of biology and genetics to the discussion of race and ethnicity demonstrates that, although scientific racism has been officially declared bogus, there is still activity in this domain. Nonetheless, the majority of scientists doing research in this field would deny that there are any racial undertones to their work. There has been an effort to separate what are presented as purely scientific rationales from all bias or prejudice. But the story is not so simple.

Although, as we have seen, great efforts have been made to go beyond the dangerous uses of racial science, some of these ideas have never really gone away. Even ideas that appear to be based on social or cultural analyses alone are actually given legitimation by a grounding in natural science. The reliance on biological or genetic research to explain human differences is another step along the way to essentializing these differences. Once this step has been taken it is very difficult to turn back and take a different route.

Politics today can be said to be overridden by the appeal to scientific justification. We can see this in the current popularity of so-called evidence-based policy: policy founded on research. At one level, this appears to be a positive move. But what does it mean when applied to areas that have traditionally been tinged by racist bias? In particular, what is the role being played by genetics in generating data on the ethnic diversity of our multicultural populations? How does this overlap with the new racist insistence on the ultimate incompatibility of black/Latino and white, or "indigenous" and "immigrant" populations?

The main story to hit the headlines in genetic research is the *human genome diversity project*. This research sets out to map human DNA sequence and has implications for debates about the relationship between humans and other animals, and the connection between diseases and certain genetic groups. All too often, the genetic groups identified in genome research overlap with traditional "racial" groups. It is difficult to know, therefore, whether this is purely coincidental or whether it is biased by the fact that race has been so predominant in ideas about human diversity. As the sociologist Robert Carter has pointed out, the problem with the project is that many of the scientists involved in it are unaware of debates in the social sciences about the socially constructed nature of race. They are also often under the false impression that the domain of scientific research is shielded from political interests.

The infiltration of politics into the supposedly neutral field of science is evident in the way people are chosen for genome research. For example, in the realm of disease identification, there is evidence that some groups – traditionally thought of as races – tend to be prone to certain diseases. For example, African-Americans have been shown to be prone to obesity and prostate cancer, among other illnesses. What this means in practice is that people who are identified as belonging to these groups (e.g. African-Americans) are then tested for the particular diseases with which the group is associated. However, as some geneticists have argued, it would be better science to look at those who actually contract disease and work from there, rather than looking for genetic similarities between those within a certain ethnic or racial group that have the disease and those who do not and making inferences about the tendency of some groups over others to develop particular diseases.

Such an approach does not take into account the social and economic factors that might be at play. For example, it is certainly legitimate to argue that African-Americans, who tend to be poorer than other groups in the United States, may suffer from obesity due to a poor, processed-food rich diet. Second, taking race and ethnicity as a baseline for genome research ignores the fact that, from a genetic point of view, there is as much variety among these groups as there is between them. In the case of African-Americans in particular, the history of the United States has revealed enough about the extent of interracial sex between masters and slaves during slavery to undermine any idea about the genetic "purity" of African-American people.

Clearly, it would be dishonest of scientists to claim that they have ignored racial categories in choosing who to do genome research on. In fact, the continuing reliance on racial categorization is based on a belief among natural scientists that race, although politically meaningless, is nonetheless biologically relevant. For example, following the drafting of the UNESCO Statement on Race and Racial Prejudice in 1950, a group of geneticists and biologists rejected the abandonment of the concept of race that the Statement's authors proposed. They drew up an alternative statement that proclaimed race as a useful concept for encapsulating what they called "heritable physical differences." They did not see any link between this and what they saw as the tendency to confuse race with nationality, religion, or culture. The problem is that, whether or not we believe that race is a useful concept, it has historically always been confused with national, religious, and cultural groupings. This ambiguous definition of what race actually refers to cannot but color the choices made by genomics researchers.

This can be clearly seen in the application of genome research to policing. DNA fingerprinting and the like are increasingly used by police in both the detection and prevention of crime. The problem with this, identified by Robert Carter, is that the application of DNA technology in policing is not unrelated to old assumptions about race. What happens is that certain populations traditionally thought to be more likely to be involved in crime, for example blacks, are being subjected to DNA testing while others are not. Obviously, under these circumstances, it is easy to draw the conclusion that blacks have a genetic propensity to crime: if DNA tests are carried out on one hundred black people convicted of crimes and they are shown to have genetic similarities, it is easy to conclude that black people are more likely to be criminals.

This leaves out of the equation the fact that institutionalized racism in policing as well as the lower socioeconomic status of many black people lead in many cases to their greater conviction for criminal offenses. The strength of genetic technology in the field of crime control is the stamp of certainty that it gives. Unlike more fuzzy social scientific arguments about the constructed nature of race and the variety of social and economic factors that lead to criminal behavior, DNA evidence appears to be plain for all to see. Genetic technology is seductively appealing in particular for governments that must be seen to be taking tough decisions in the face of mounting violence, crime, and terrorism. Carter calls this "genetic reductionism," or the idea that we can know all we need to know by looking into our DNA. The problem is that if DNA testing is not applied universally to everyone regardless of their so-called racial identity, it remains of little use beyond being a very powerful means of reinforcing preexisting ideas about race.

Taken together, Barker's analysis of the "new racism" and contemporary genetic technologies can be seen as being part of an overall drive to cement the idea of human variation in what is portrayed as a nonracial way. What do I mean by this? The culturalism of the new racism claims to reject the old hierarchies of race while, at the same time, insisting on the inherent incompatibility between groups of human beings from various parts of the world. As we have seen, like racialization, culturalization essentializes the differences between human beings and sees them as unchangeable and inherent. However, because it openly rejects the label of race, even going as far as to argue that we are living in a post-racial or raceless age, it avoids the charge of racism.

Similarly, the proponents of genetics as the tool *par excellence* for explaining why we are the way we are claim that they are utterly unmotivated by racism. However, because of the insistence by biologists and geneticists both that race is a scientifically useful category and that they are entirely uninfluenced by politics, they – perhaps unknowingly – end up reinforcing racist preconceptions. In particular, funding for genome research in the areas of disease identification and policing has been motivated by such preconceptions, particularly about the tendency of groups traditionally thought of as racial to be involved in certain types of crime. Scientists who rely on such funding cannot, therefore, claim to be ignorant of the political implications of their work.

Clearly racial science continues to exist albeit under a different guise, one that claims to be non-racist. It can thrive in a culture that promotes the idea that it is post-race, or even raceless, while in fact reinforcing some of the most potent stereotypes associated with old-fashioned racism. To understand the formulation of racism today, it is necessary to understand this paradox. It is not a carefully worked-out conspiracy. Rather, it is the consequence of failing to deal with the political, social, and cultural legacies of racism on our societies and of brushing them under the carpet without getting rid of some of their core assumptions. It is as if by vociferously denying any connection to race, the politics of immigration, policing, or genomic research will automatically be freed from their *de facto* association with it. If anything, the conviction with which many of those in government and in the world of scientific research hold up their anti-racist credentials is proof of how much the idea of race has embedded itself in the structures of science and politics.

5

The specter of immigration in the shadow of the war on terror

[T]he war on asylum and the "war on terror" – one, the unarmed invasion, the other, the armed enemy within, has produced the idea of a nation under siege, and, on the ground, a racism that cannot tell a settler from an immigrant, an asylum seeker from a Muslim, a Muslim from a terrorist. All of us non-whites, at first sight, are terrorists or illegals. We wear our passports on our faces.

A. Sivanandan (2007: 48)

This final chapter looks at what racism means in the first decade of the twenty-first century and at how racism today is bound up with the creation of the *image* that there are irreconcilable differences between "cultures" and "civilizations," both globally and on the domestic level. The idea that there is a clash of civilizations, famously suggested by the American conservative political scientist Samuel Huntington in 1994, has had a profound impact on global politics. It is dictating policies that are undeniably related to racism, such as the wars and occupations of Iraq and Afghanistan, and their domestic effects, immigration policy, civil liberties legislation, and the future of multiculturalism.

Since September 11, 2001, the idea that a new world order, defined by the agenda of terrorists set on destroying the Western world, has influenced how we all live our lives. Significant changes in the way democratic states in the West are run have been made in response to what is seen as the threat from outsiders with dangerous agendas. These outsiders can be divided into three groups: "immigrants and asylum seekers," "terrorists," and "Muslims." Just who belongs to each group is not clearly defined. For example, terrorists are those such as the members of the Al Qaeda network and other extremist "Islamist" organizations who threaten our security.

However, there is significant confusion over whether they are foreign immigrants or citizens of Western countries. Muslims in general have been identified with terrorism, be they Western citizens, migrants to the West, or Iraqi "insurgents." Immigrants and asylum seekers too have been portrayed by both governments and the media as potential terrorists and as a threat to the national social fabric and to indigenous workers alike. The power of anti-terrorism discourse leads to whole groups of highly diverse people being simplistically classified as either terrorist, Muslim, or immigrant. It does not really matter what are the vast differences between those who are defined under one, or all three, of these labels. Increasingly, any variation between them is seen as negligible.

In this chapter, I look at how this apparently new discourse is a continuation of some of the central themes of racism and racialization. Although we can say that we are living through particularly critical times that seem to be marked by a profound mistrust of the Other, there are many parallels between today's obsession with the figure of the Muslim terrorist and the antisemitism of 1930s Europe. Likewise, there are similarities between the idea of a global clash of civilizations, which legitimizes foreign invasions such as those of Iraq and Afghanistan, and old-fashioned imperialism.

This chapter focuses on three interrelated themes that demonstrate how the specific ways in which racism is played out today also encompass all the elements of racism dealt with throughout the book. The first section examines anti-terrorism and the racialized politics of fear that dominates the political sphere today. In the second section, I draw a red line to contemporary immigration policies of Western states to show how they are aligned with a new racializing discourse that, rather than simply dividing the West from "the rest," now separates globally between rich and poor, productive and unproductive. In the concluding section, I turn to the impact that global racisms in the spheres of terrorism and migration have on the racialized in Western societies and ask what future is there for multiculturalism?

Racism and the "war on terror"

It is now a cliché to say that the world changed forever on September 11, 2001. Although it may seem that politics were radically transformed on that day, a lot of these seemingly fundamental changes were not so much changes as exacerbations of existing conditions. The way in which minority groups, Muslims in particular, have been targeted by the so-called war on terror is reminiscent of racisms past. The result, now like before, is the scapegoating of a whole diversity of individuals and groups all loosely associated in one way or another with what we call terrorism and seen as a fundamental threat to our existence.

There is no doubt that the way in which the United States and its allies decided to react to the terrorist attacks of September 2001 on New York and Washington – the invasions of Iraq and Afghanistan – have led to a growth in racism. It is racism on a global scale, because the war on terror is predicated on the idea of the world as divided into "good" and "evil," democratic and so-called rogue states.

This clash of civilizations between friends and enemies has been reproduced on home territory. The fight against terror is linked to the debate over immigration and multiculturalism, for it does not only concern fighting insurgents in Iraq or Afghanistan, it is also about which of our neighbors it is safe to live beside. The war on terror, in both its global and its local manifestations, is wholly racialized. It is based on a racialized worldview and has racist outcomes. Several aspects are of particular significance: the construction of the image of the "fundamentalist Muslim terrorist," the reduction of politics to the balance between fear and security, and the impact on the lives of ordinary people caught in the crossfire.

The roots of the complex relationship between Islam and the West can be found in the historical relationship to the "Orient." In his book, *Orientalism*, the Palestinian scholar Edward Said sets out the thesis that the West constructs the East as wholly other and inferior, representing everything that "we" are not. He saw Orientalism as an argument against humanist values because it constructs the East as being outside the sphere of humanity. This contributes to creating an "us" and "them" divide between the West and the "Muslim world" that ultimately sees the latter as beyond the confines of humanity. Islam, as the religion of the Orient, is thus regarded as subordinate to Christianity and/or Western rationality. From the early conquests of the Middle East to the later exploitation of its most valuable resource, oil, the Orient has been the target of the West's crusade to dominate it.

Like racialization, Orientalism works along parallel lines of contempt and fascination. The Orient was reviled as primitive and dangerous, yet was also secretly coveted. Fantasies, particularly about the exotic and mysterious nature of its "beguiling" women, are a prominent feature of Orientalist literature. This theme continues in contemporary discourses about the Muslim veil, which is portrayed in the West both as a mark of patriarchal domination and as an intriguing symbol of the potential female mysteries it conceals.

Today, the Muslim veil has become a shorthand for the view of Muslims as impenetrable strangers in our midst. The invasion of Afghanistan by US-led forces in late 2001 was accompanied by a global campaign for the rights of Afghan women who had been the victims of terrible abuse at the hands not only of the Taliban government, but of patriarchal Afghan society as a whole. *Elle* magazine helped three Afghan women to escape the Taliban regime in order to tell their stories to the West. This instigated a flurry of campaigns to help Afghan women come out from under the yoke of oppression. Feminists and anti-racists have pointed out the double standards such campaigns promote because they have created a tenuous link between the plight of Afghan women and more general assumptions about Muslim women the world over.

Muslim women who wear the veil are generally perceived as having been forced to do so, and Islam is seen as a religion that oppresses women as a matter of course. A tenuous connection is made between the enforcement of the veil and the whole gamut of aggression against women, from domestic violence to genital mutilation to honor killings. The specificities of these crimes notwithstanding (genital mutilation for example originates as tribal African practice rather than an Islamic one), Muslim women are seen as having no choice over their own fate.

It is unquestionable that there is a rise in the spread of religiosity among Muslims worldwide. One of the reasons for this is the reaction to what is seen as the immorality of Western consumerism and the unbridled spread of the neo-liberal capitalist model. A symbol of this consumerism is the use of images of women in highly sexualized poses to advertise a range of goods and services, long criticized by Western feminists. Many religious Muslim women feel that wearing the veil is a stance against the tendency to objectify and thus denigrate women. Moreover, the veil is seen by many Muslim women as a visible protest against the victimization of Muslims around the globe. The occupation of the Palestinian territories by Israel, the failure of the West to intervene to stop genocide in Bosnia, the sanctions against Iraq in the 1990s leading to the deaths of up to a million people are all catalysts in the trend towards a return to religious ways of life and, for a minority, the embracing of radicalism. This may be exacerbated by policies that deny individuals the right to wear the *hijab*. For example, according to Florida law, veiled Muslim women must be photographed for their driver's license with their heads uncovered. A woman who sued in 2003 failed to see her right to the free exercise of religion upheld by the Florida court. Condemnation of the veil in France led in 2004 to the passing of a law making it an offense to wear "ostensible religious symbols" in public institutions such as schools and government offices. In Britain in 2007, a prominent politician, Jack Straw, asked a Muslim woman who came to his constituency office to remove her *niqab* (face veil) if she wished to talk to him. Straw called the veil a "visible statement of separation and difference."

The image of the terrorist is indelibly printed on the minds of everyone who has ever watched television, read a newspaper, or surfed the Internet. It is the bearded, *kaffiya*-clad, or turbaned young man, clutching a Kalashnikov, perhaps with a belt laden with explosives strapped to his waist, a Koran open in his hands. This image spells danger, and the prospect of death and destruction it conjures up scares us half to death! As Chris Sparks notes, both the protagonists of terror and those who fight them are involved in producing this fear-inducing image. On the one hand, the self-proclaimed *jihadists* know that the image of a would-be suicide bomber or an Al Qaeda leader, broadcast around the world at the click of a mouse, instills fear and dread in the hearts of its Western audience. They play on it because they know that never before have those who dare to oppose Western hegemony had the power to terrify to such an extent. The fear is often greater than the result of the threat they wield. On the other hand, Western governments and media use the same image to make that fear concrete. Legitimized by the words and policies of the US-led alliance, the consequences for our personal safety of the actions of terrorists shake us to our core.

The idea that Muslims are less concerned with the preservation of human life is a central myth in the creation of the fear that has gripped Western societies since 9/11. Suicide bombers are portrayed as unstoppable and as ready to strike at any time because they are unconcerned for their own lives. They will kill themselves as they kill us.

Never before has the West had to contend with such a formidable threat. In the United States, a country that had never been successfully invaded by a foreign enemy, the power of the suicide bomber to wield destruction is the stuff of nightmares. The way in which fear induced by the terrorist threat has become the cornerstone of a fundamental change to politics has consequences for the interpretation of racism today. The fear that danger is everywhere and imminent is a central theme of the war on terror.

Politics has therefore been turned from a proactive process into a reactive one. We are presented with the scenario that our lives are in almost constant danger. This is represented by the alerts – yellow, orange, red – that represent the severity of the threat at various times. The job of government and law enforcement is to attempt to stop potential disasters such as 9/11 or the Madrid and London bombings from occurring again, by any means necessary. The primary aim of politics has become ensuring national security. Security is based on creating a separation between insiders and outsiders with only those who are within the nation protected. Increasingly, *who* is categorized as belonging to the nation is ethnically defined. The lessons of the bombings in London on July 7, 2005, are that "terrorists" are not beyond attacking their fellow citizens.

The politics of fear, therefore, are built not only upon an "us and them" mentality that separates between those located in geographically different spaces. On the contrary, just like antisemitism, the enemy most feared is that within. Although before the London bombings, immigrants and foreign nationals were seen as most likely to be terrorist suspects, now Muslims who are citizens or residents of our countries are looked upon with the most fear. The war on terror, as it is fought on the home front, is targeted against the man who sits beside us as we take the bus home, the veiled woman we pass in the supermarket aisle, or the bearded man on his way to the mosque.

The consequence of the extent to which fear has come to govern us is in its impact on policy. It is now taken for granted that whenever we travel we undergo longer and more arduous checks. The politics of fear numb us into accepting that this is just something we must endure in the interests of our safety. But what is the impact of such heightened security measures on those of us who fit the profile of what a terrorist might look like?

Racial or ethnic profiling is not a new policing tactic. The expression "driving while black" describes the greater tendency of police to stop black drivers for random searches. Stop and search measures have been a feature of policing in many countries, as they were during colonial times and in racial regimes such as that of apartheid South Africa. Stop and search is dissociable from the assumptions of racialization. Because black, and now Muslim or "Muslim-looking," youths are portrayed in popular culture as being more likely to be involved in crime, they are also more likely to be stopped, searched, and arrested.

Racial or ethnic profiling does not mean using a person's skin color or ethnic background in order to identify them. Instead, profiling "involves reliance on a *generalization* about people of a particular group" (Cole 2003: 53) for the purposes of incrimination. So profiling leads to policing based on the generalized assumption that Muslim men are more likely to be terrorists than for example white women, to the exclusion of all other groups. The police spotlight is almost exclusively on a restricted group of people. However, because Islam is a religion rather than an ethnicity, profiling relies on a very crude approximation of what Muslims are most likely to look like. In the United States, because all those who allegedly carried out the 9/11 attacks were Arab, the focus is mainly on people who in the popular perception "look Arab."

As David Cole reminds us, this way of going about things leads to the incrimination of an enormous group of people all over the world because they happen to have similar features to a tiny minority of individuals who happen to be terrorists. Anecdotes abound of people being mistaken for Arabs or Muslims, leading tragically even to their being killed in reprisal attacks for the events of 9/11. One such case is that of Balbir Singh Sodhi who was gunned down on September 15, 2001, in Mesa, Arizona. The turban-wearing Sikh was killed outside his gas station. Sodhi's killer spent the hours before the murder in a bar, uttering racist epithets, and bragging of his intention to kill those "responsible for September 11." Profiling leads to the racialization of an entire group of people as terrorists. The fact that it is a fundamental dimension of policing for national security gives the stamp of legitimacy to the assumptions made by the killers of Balbir Singh and those like them.

The situation in which the West has been placed as a result of international terrorism is presented as being completely unprecedented. The idea that the threat is constant and that its full extent is unknown drives *government measures*. The attacks on Afghanistan and Iraq were preemptive rather than reactive. According to the US-led military alliance, they were necessary to prevent the potential threat originating in these countries. Preemptive military action is one in a range of extraordinary measures that have been put in place as part of the war on terror. How are these measures associated with racism?

The Italian philosopher Giorgio Agamben introduced the idea of "state of exception" in order to describe special measures taken by governments that suspend the rule of law. The most clear historical example of the state of exception is Germany under Nazism. The state of exception legitimates violence, exclusion, and the violation of liberty and rights. It provides a division between friends and enemies, between "civilized" and "barbarians," "progressive" and "pre-modern." In other words, it divides between those who must be protected by law and those deemed unworthy of this protection. The modern rule of law is based on the principle that each individual is a legal subject. The state of exception thus rejects this fundamental principle. By placing some individuals beyond the law, they are basically reduced to a status of inhumanity, because it is this legal status of the individual that binds people across the globe in their humanity, as equal subjects before the law. The idea that there are those who are within and those who are beyond the law is central to the war against terror, bringing about what some see as a permanent state of exception. Agamben argues that US-led exceptionalism has led to the erasure of the legal status of individuals. Countless numbers of people have been placed beyond the law, denied the right to a fair trial under any system.

This has been achieved through the establishing of special prisons such as that at Guantánamo Bay in Cuba or at Kandahar and Bagram in Afghanistan. From 2001 on, individuals have been picked up off the streets in places like Pakistan or Afghanistan, most often sold to the US-led forces for $5,000, and imprisoned in places that few even know exist. Above all, the policy of so-called extraordinary rendition has allowed for thousands to disappear, mainly to prisons in countries such as Egypt or Morocco where torture is part of the daily routine.

Extraordinary rendition is the embodiment of the divide between "us" and the "evil-doers," as George Bush famously put it, that underpins the war on terror. It is extraordinary because it allows for laws enshrined in the US statutes to be bypassed by the use of "third countries." By sending suspects to prisons in other countries, the US can turn a legal blind eye to their treatment and ensure that they have no access to a fair trial on US soil, the country with the ultimate legal responsibility for their conviction as terrorists. The term used to describe those who disappear through extraordinary rendition is "enemy combatant." This categorization legitimizes the imprisonment, torture, and often the killing of those it labels because, it is claimed, the threat posed by international terrorism creates a necessary state of exception in which all is permitted.

Nevertheless, the very existence of extraordinary rendition recognizes the fact that the rule of law cannot be universally contravened. It would be impossible for the type of treatment meted out to enemy combatants in foreign prisons to occur on United States territory because, according to US law, the charging of a suspect for a crime must end in her being granted a fair hearing. Extraordinary rendition admits that there are two categories of people, those within the sphere of law and those without it. Generally, those within the sphere of law are citizens of the US, its allies, or other "democratic" countries. However, this principle has been contravened when citizens are found in areas of the world where the rule is applied less stringently, as was the case of the so-called Tipton Three – Ruhal Ahmed, Asif Iqbal and Shafiq Rasul – British citizens picked up in Afghanistan while visiting the country as war broke out in 2001. Found in Afghanistan on the eve of the coalition's invasion, it appeared that they must have been involved in terrorism. The three were imprisoned in Guantánamo for two years before being released without charge. British-born sons of Pakistani and Bangladeshi Muslims, they would almost definitely not have undergone the same treatment had they not been of Muslim descent.

The treatment of "enemy combatants" in Guantánamo Bay and the other prisons used to hold them indefinitely in locations around the world has come to light in the wider world. In 2004, the torture of Iraqi prisoners by US guards at Abu Ghraib prison was splashed across the global media. The image of a man forced to stand naked on a box with a black hood over his head, his arms splayed and electric wires crisscrossing his body, has become the symbol of the failed US invasion of Iraq. This picture and many others showing the physical and sexual tormenting of prisoners were taken by US soldiers, used as screen savers and exchanged by e-mail before being revealed to the world at large.

OCTOBER 17, 1961

The events of October 17, 1961, in Paris are an historical example of the dehumanizing treatment of those seen as terrorists during another war between the West and the Muslim world: the Algerian war of independence. Algerian immigrants were living in France in their thousands by this time and many were loyal to the *Front de Libération National* (FLN), the anti-colonialist Algerian force. Many attacks against Algerians in France were carried out during the preceding months by the *Organisation armée secrète* (OAS) led by the former Nazi collaborator, Maurice Papon. In October, Papon issued a special curfew that applied only to Algerians in France in order, it stated, "to put an end promptly to the criminal acts of the terrorists." On October 17, the FLN decided to boycott the curfew and called its supporters to a peaceful demonstration in Paris. Its aim was to highlight publicly the level of repression against Algerians. It was met with police batons. On the bridges of Paris, police beat the demonstrators into the waters of the Seine. Ten thousand others were arrested and taken to pre-planned custody centers where they were subjected to further beatings. An unknown number of Algerians were summarily executed. To this day the precise number of victims remains unknown, although some two to three hundred are said to have lost their lives. The French government rigidly controlled information about the events from the outset. Newspapers and film footage were censored, cameras confiscated, access to the detention centers forbidden to journalists, and eyewitnesses silenced with threats of prosecution. It was not until 1997 that an inquiry and limited access to police archives were permitted by the French government. There has been no official admission of the crimes committed on behalf of the state. The incident goes almost unknown by the majority of the French population. The curfew against Algerians in France led directly to the common association that persists to this day between "Algerian"and "criminal." The dehumanization of Algerians by the French regime to the extent that they could be killed and drowned in the center of Paris and that almost no one was aware or concerned is evidence of the extent of racism's repercussions.

As David Cole notes, it is not that the treatment meted out to Abu Ghraib's prisoners was specifically ordered. Rather, the abuse was made possible because of the predominance of the racist idea that they were less than human. By insisting on the division of the world into civilized and uncivilized, good and evil, the rhetoric of the war on terror establishes the idea that those imprisoned, tortured, and killed are not like us. Torturing an Iraqi insurgent, a "terrorist," is not the same as torturing a US soldier or killing a Spanish civilian. The lives of the former are rendered less worthy because of the presumption that they are intent on destroying "us." The inhumanity of the enemy extends to everyone who is seen as belonging to the same group; in this case Muslims worldwide. This racialized logic leads to:

> treating some − foreign nationals, and especially in the present crisis, Arabs and Muslims − as less deserving of liberty, less *human*, than the rest of us. When we selectively deny basic rights to members of a group based on their identity as different from (and less powerful than) us, we deny their common humanity. (Cole 2003: xv)

Immigration and "xeno-racism"

Migrants from poverty-stricken countries are regularly reported to be literally invading our shores. From the US to Australia and from Denmark to Italy, there is a growing consensus that "enough is enough": the West has been too generous in the past; it must now put a stop to "absurd levels" of immigration. Although most of the media-fueled hysteria regarding immigration is based on incorrect or exaggerated figures, it has motivated the general belief that immigration has spiraled out of control.

Certainly the numbers of asylum seekers and "economic migrants" from across the globe saw a marked increase in the 1990s and the early 2000s. This has now evened out for reasons that include the toughened response of governments in the face of so-called illegal immigration, but also a manipulation of statistics that blurs the lines between what politicians are eager to present as "bona fide" versus "bogus" migrants. I examine how these new divisions between categories of migrants relate to racialization and the creation of a new type of racism that A. Sivanandan has called xeno-racism.

Who exactly do we mean when we speak of "immigrants"? Racism has not only been directed against those who migrated themselves. It can also affect the generations descended from them. However, not all immigrants are faced with racism. Groups of immigrants to the US such as the Irish, who faced discrimination upon arrival, soon rose through the racial ranks due to their participation in the oppression of blacks. There is a clear hierarchy among immigrant communities that differs from country to country, depending on its particular history. Historically, black migrants and those from the poorer regions of the world have fared worse than others, and immigrants have been pitted against the indigenous peoples of North America, Australia, and New Zealand. Today poverty, often in conjunction with skin color, distinguishes between "productive" migrants and those deemed "unworthy."

The presence of significant numbers of what are known as ethnic minorities throughout the developed world has changed our societies indelibly. This is particularly so in the towns and cities where the first immigrants chose to settle and where large communities have since developed. In major cities such as New York, Toronto, Marseille, or Berlin the city itself has undergone a major transformation because such a large proportion of the population is of immigrant origin. In these cities, not only are some neighborhoods inhabited by particular communities, but whole cities are veritable multicultural metropolises. As a result, people from all walks of life are now familiar with a range of cuisines from across the globe, and music such as bhangra or reggae has long since entered the mainstream. However, when we contrast the realm of culture to that of the job market, the continuing discrimination against those of immigrant background is clear. Black and brown people originating in Europe's former colonies have always been faced with institutionalized racism in employment and education.

Popular discourse usually focuses on particular groups of people when others are described as "immigrants" or "ethnic minorities." The immigrant melting-pot of the United States is nonetheless hierarchically organized. White Protestant culture is dominant and all other groups are subordinate to it. In both common discourse and government policy, just who is considered an "immigrant" is highly selective and does not cover the whole range of people who, in legal terms, fall under this category. For example, two million Irish illegal immigrants in the US were given amnesty in 1986, leading to six times that many illegally entering the US in the years thereafter. In December 2007, the Irish government asked the US to legalize Irish immigrants in a move that would put Irish illegals at an advantage over their counterparts from other non-Western countries. In contrast, militia-style "Minute Men" have taken to patrolling the US-Mexican border to thwart illegals attempting to enter the country. This is based on the belief that Latino migration is threatening the very heart of the United States with the aim of altering it beyond recognition.

This traditional association of "immigrants" with non-whites has undergone significant change in more recent times following the end of the Cold War. The term "immigrant" now acts as a divider between rich and poor on a global scale. Many from countries in the rich world can choose to travel around the globe, settling where they like, while those who migrate from the poor world are seen as attempting to take away what is rightfully ours: our jobs and our culture. The division of the globe in the 1950s into first, second, and third worlds is at the heart of this separation into rich and poor that dictates who can enter and who is kept at the gates. Three-world theory creates "us" and "them" divisions on a global scale, creating in-nations and out-nations, those to whom we extend a welcome and those whom we shut out.

At the start of the twentieth century in the US, and following the Second World War in Europe, immigrants were welcomed, necessary as they were for the economy and infrastructure of many countries. Government policy dictating whether or not they could enter and stay changed as the need for migrant work began to conflict with the political interests of those in power. A line can be traced from the early decades that followed the Second World War to the present revealing how government policy has institutionalized racism against immigrants and their descendants. Successive governments' attitudes also demonstrate how the debate on immigration has changed in the wake of globalization to create new discourses of anti-immigrant racism based on the racialization of poverty.

The "problem" of immigration began when it could no longer be confined to the domain of labor and economics. It was soon realized that migration was not anonymous; human beings were involved and human beings had to live, eat, be educated, be treated if they were ill, and have places to shop, worship, and socialize. Immigrant communities had become installed in many Western towns and cities but there was still no real consciousness of the fact that they were, for the most part, there for good. The predominance of nationalism and the myth of cultural homogeneity made immigrants seem alien and threatening. It was also in the interests of governments to create two-tiered systems that divided between citizens and immigrants. While in some countries, such as the US, the ease with which citizenship could be acquired meant a less officialized racism against non-white migrants, in other countries, such as Switzerland and Germany, the division was clear. The Turkish *gäst arbeiter* in Germany, for example, retained the status of guest workers and even their German-born children were refused nationality until a change in the law in 1999.

The difficulty of integrating immigrants into mainstream society is often seen as due to the disparity between their way of life and that of the "host" country. Immigrants have always been portrayed as having a different set of moral values from those of the locals. However, creating the conditions of integration is a difficult challenge that demands a shift in thinking about what or who *constitutes* a nation. It has therefore been easier for governments to comply with the view that immigrants refuse to integrate and to use this as justification for curbing future immigration. Criminality among black youths, for example, has been used as a reason for stopping immigration of people from Africa and the Caribbean. However, such a debate generally conceals the reasons for criminality that cover a whole complex of factors including unemployment, racist policing, and the tendency of the judiciary to hand out harsher sentences to blacks. Similarly, a common complaint is that immigrants "refuse" to speak the language of the "host" nation. However, this complaint does not take into account whether or not immigrants, especially women and the elderly, have access to language classes provided by the government that sees fluency in English or German as a condition of integration.

Not only have immigrants been reprimanded for failing to integrate, the blame for racism has also been pinned on them. Paradoxically, the existence and spread of racist attitudes has been proposed as being one of the main reasons for curbing immigration. Although immigrants do not take away jobs and welfare from citizens because they generally work for the lowest pay and in the poorest of conditions, the common perception, fueled by government action, is that they are "scroungers" and that the racism they face is par for the course. Because racism reflects badly on a society as a whole, the logic is that in order to avoid it, immigration must be strictly controlled. Tough immigration laws in Europe, for example, have turned the European Union into a veritable fortress with those outside left clamoring at the gates.

Although unfettered labor migration to the First World was virtually a thing of the past by the 1970s, the West continued to allow restricted numbers of migrants claiming asylum from oppressive foreign regimes to enter and settle. The right to claim asylum is enshrined in the 1951 Geneva Convention on Refugees. The Convention was drawn up in light of the refugee crisis in Europe following the end of the Second World War when millions of displaced persons were hoarded into refugee camps. The terrible outcome of the war made it incumbent upon the richer states to protect those fleeing from torture, oppression, starvation, or conflict. Wars such as that in Korea in the 1950s or Vietnam in the 1960s, or events in many of the famine-infested regions of Africa throughout the last sixty years have seen refugees displaced all over the world. The great majority of the world's refugee population is located within their own countries or regions. Only a handful of refugees ever make it to Western shores.

Until the 1970s, refugees were accepted by governments as part of designated programs of aid. From the 1970s on, both the rise in conflict in many regions and the greater ease of international travel led to higher numbers of people arriving in the West to claim asylum. The principles of the Geneva Convention meant that governments had the responsibility to grant them asylum until it could be verified whether or not they qualified for refugee status. However, the drafters of the Geneva Convention and the governments that signed it had only European displaced persons in mind. While the Convention referred to universal principles, it was never intended to cope with masses of non-white people from former colonial lands demanding protection from human rights abuses, hunger, and war.

The rise in asylum seekers to the West during the 1980s, going, in Europe, from seventy thousand in 1983 to two hundred thousand in 1989, coincided with the clampdown on labor migration. Many governments suspected that would-be "economic migrants" were choosing the asylum route, inventing reasons for claiming refugee status. This led gradually to the current policy: the almost universal withdrawal of asylum rights and the criminalization of asylum seekers as "bogus" economic migrants in disguise. According to a report by the UNHCR in 2006, asylum figures fell globally over the previous five years. Whereas the numbers have been dropping consistently across all countries, Australia, Canada, New Zealand, and the United States receive fewer asylum seekers per capita than Europe. While Western governments have been quick to portray this as a success, the UNHCR claims that "industrialized countries should be asking themselves whether by imposing ever tighter restrictions on asylum seekers they are not closing their doors to men, women and children fleeing persecution."

The distinction between forced and economic migration is itself antiquarian. Forced migration traditionally refers to those literally forced to leave their countries because their lives were at risk. Examples abound over the course of the second half of the twentieth century of political refugees from violent and anti-democratic regimes from Iran to Chile. However, with the rising prevalence of ethnic conflict, famine, and economic degradation in countries as diverse as Ethiopia, Sudan, Bosnia, or Iraq, the boundary between those forced to flee for political or economic reasons became blurred. How was it possible to argue that someone fleeing starvation was not a forced migrant?

Today it appears that the very mention of asylum seekers or immigrants is met with contempt. The policy of detaining failed asylum seekers and "illegals" in Immigration Detention Centers and deporting them to their country of origin supports the idea that it is time to "get tough" on immigrants. Yet these harsh policies do not deter those fleeing persecution or seeking out a better existence who are desperate to get in. Regularly, would-be immigrants from Mexico are guided over the border into the US under the watchful gaze of border police and vigilantes. Those who wish to reach the UK risk their lives by attempting to pass through the Channel Tunnel from France clinging to the underside of high-speed Eurostar trains. Similarly, African or East European migrants, having traveled thousands of miles, including many on foot, set out in small rubber boats hoping to reach the coasts of Spain or Italy. Hundreds of bodies of those for whom high seas, dehydration, sickness, or unscrupulous traffickers proved too much dot the seas. Hundreds more are discovered too late as bloated bodies wash up onto sandy beaches.

The prevalent view of migrants as posing an almost insurmountable problem that must be overcome at all costs to ensure the survival of the

West is in fact an artificial one based on old ideas about immigration. In the popular imagination, immigration poses an ethno-racial problem. The difficulty of integrating immigrants is presented as the reason why it is necessary to bring primary immigration to a stop. However, the situation has been dramatically transformed since then. The changing nature of industry and manufacturing brought about by economic globalization, the resultant prosperity, and a declining birthrate all mean that the West needs migrant labor as never before. Nonetheless, the industrialized world is also confronted with a security situation that dictates that it maintains strong borders. Just who is permitted to immigrate is therefore held up to extremely close scrutiny. In response, governments are moving to introduce policies of *managed migration*. These policies are based not on a classical ethno-racial division of the world into developed and underdeveloped nations. It is a much more individualized policy that discriminates between rich and poor on a global scale and targets poor white migrants as much as it does poor black ones. It is what the A. Sivanandan has dubbed xeno-racism.

Managed, or chosen, migration is the attempt to systematize a number of ad hoc practices that are already in operation in most Western countries. Today, illegal migrants or those on very short-term visas work in a variety of badly paid and often difficult jobs as pickers, cleaners, and laborers. They are generally denied social security rights, work inhumane hours, often in several different jobs, and live in cramped, unhygienic conditions. They are at the mercy of employers who dictate when and if they will work. They live in constant fear of the immigration authorities who may imprison them in detention centers and deport them.

Managed migration is based on the recognition that migrant labor is a necessary function of the conditions of the knowledge-based economy. Governments' retraction of full financing from a range of publicly funded sectors such as health and transport means that recruitment must look beyond national borders in the hunt for those willing to do the job for less pay. Likewise, the service industry generated by the overspill of wealth from the global economy needs fueling by an ever-growing army of menial workers. More money in the economy demands the building of more roads, houses, and offices, and hence bodies are needed to lift, carry, and construct. In short, the growth of neo-liberal economies is predicated on competition and gains are generated by getting the job done for less. What this literally means is that if local people refuse to do the job for the pay offered, there are many from further afield who would jump at the chance.

Yet rather than look to migrants and asylum seekers already present in Western countries, managed migration combines economic and political reasoning. It is based on ensuring that today's migrant workers will not make the same demands as their predecessors and damage the delicate balance of "race relations." Instead a new global approach to migration management is being put in place. Managed migration is based on the creation of a tiered approach to immigration. At the top of the hierarchy are skilled workers, recruited for jobs in IT or, most frequently, medicine. They are hand-picked for the role on the basis not only of their competency but also of their capacity for integration. It is therefore a system that racializes poverty. Global migration management is like a "socioeconomic Social Darwinism that allows the First World to maintain its economic dominance by emptying the poorer worlds of their skilled workforces" (Fekete 2001: 29).

At the bottom of the scale, the global regime of managed migration functions by beginning way beyond the borders of Western countries. As Fekete explains, managed migration is made possible by cooperation between power blocs with shared interests and international organizations set up for the purpose such as the International Organization for Migration. Their consolidated approach leads to immigration checks taking place at the point of departure rather than of arrival, weeding undesirables out before they ever set foot on Western territory. This clearly makes it impossible for would-be refugees to claim asylum as they can only do so on entry into the country from which protection is being sought. To fill the quotas of necessary unskilled labor, workers are offered short-term temporary contracts. Laws restrict the duration and number of times an individual can enter the country, forcing migrants to return home between contracts. This measure is a purposeful means of stopping foreign migrants from settling in the country. The system leads a great many into a clandestine existence in which they are constantly prey to immigration police and profiteering employers if not abject poverty.

The managed migration scheme leads in effect to the criminalization of unsolicited migration. However, because it is accompanied by an almost complete retraction of the rights to seek asylum, those who

THE STRAWBERRY PICKERS OF HUELVA

The Spanish province of Huelva grows a large proportion of Europe's strawberries, and employs fifty-five thousand people annually. In 2001, ten thousand of these were undocumented migrants, mainly from Morocco. In 2001, they began a campaign for regularization with the help of local trade unions. As a result, although the campaign was relatively successful, the government issued only a restricted number of work permits to African workers and sought strawberry pickers from Romania and Poland, mainly women, instead. Because the African workers had successfully campaigned for regularization, employers preferred to hire undocumented labor from elsewhere because such newcomers would be less likely to demand their rights. The North African workers found themselves confronted by an absurd situation. At the beginning of the 2002 season they were there waiting for the work to begin. Much to their surprise, they saw thousands of young Polish and Romanian women arrive who began picking strawberries, often for less money than the Moroccans would have received. This left the Moroccans in a state of poverty, often living in the streets, without shelter, food, or water. The situation became extremely tense, giving rise to a wave of racism against the Moroccans, who were seen as dirty and lazy. Four thousand local people demonstrated in Huelva against "civil insecurity." For the first time in Andalusia, the extreme right-wing National Democracy Party displayed their posters widely. Despite restrictions, the Moroccans, desperate for any work and unable to go elsewhere, stayed in the region. Whenever there was a particularly big harvest, or on Sundays or religious holidays, the employers could turn to this reserve army of laborers whom they paid miserable wages in humiliating conditions. At the end of the season the employers stated with satisfaction that it had been one of the most profitable so far.

The Seattle Public Library
Douglass-Truth Branch
Visit us on the Web: www.spl.org

Check out date: 01/10/16

xxxxxxxxxxxx3642

Racism and ethnic bias : everybody's
book
0010043131928   Due date: 01/31/16

Racism and ethnic discrimination /
00100097446   Due date: 01/31/16
book]

ITEMS: 2

Renewals: 206-386-4190
TeleCirc: 206-386-9015 / 24 hours a day
Online myaccount.spl.org

* * * * * * * * * * * * * *

Pay your fines/fees online at pay.spl.org

are labeled criminal illegal immigrants are most often those most in need of protection. The rhetoric against illegal immigration also bemoans the spread of human trafficking. The criminal activities of traffickers organized in global networks force would-be migrants to pay extortionate sums to secure their passage to the West. Many die in the process, abandoned by unscrupulous traffickers or falling prey to the countless hardships of the grueling journey. The case of fifty-eight Chinese migrants who died, suffocated to death in the airless container of a truck in Dover in the UK in 2000, is testament to the lengths many will go to attempt to enter. The spread of trafficking is a direct result of the clampdown on the legal channels for seeking asylum and the stringency of managed migration policies.

Those who put their lives in the hands of traffickers and who go underground are representatives of the poor majority world within the rich world, those whom as Zygmunt Bauman has remarked are seen as "wasted lives." According to A. Sivanandan, the new xeno-racism of the global era is brought into play by the logic that drives managed migration. That logic is one that divides the globe into the haves and the have-nots, no longer distinguishing between people on the sole basis of the color of their skin. Under this rubric, the poor of the ex-Soviet Union and its satellite states – Albanians, Poles, or Roma gypsies – are as alien as the African with whom they may find themselves sharing a dormitory in an Immigration Detention Center awaiting deportation. The new xeno-racism is excused as xenophobia, a natural fear of the other. However, it works in the same way as racializing practices do to essentialize all those deemed undesirable because they come, it is claimed, to take away our jobs, steal our homes, and transform our way of life.

Xeno-racism can be seen as part of an overall logic that governs the post-Communist world. The end of the Cold War brought with it the demise of the West's "natural enemy," state socialism. The unipolarity of global political power, the fact that the United States is now the world's only superpower, does not mean that the West no longer needs enemies. Today, the enemies of the West are the poor and the migrants. As Gargi Bhattacharyya argues, the old racisms practiced by individual states are now harnessed to a global political project and recreated therein on an unprecedented scale. This has a direct effect both on the lives of immigrants and would-be asylum seekers, as well as on ethnic minority communities settled in Western countries. This new globalized racism is mediated by and connected to the "war on terror."

The new assimilation

Tough responses to immigration, the retraction of the rights of asylum seekers, and the scapegoating of outsiders as part of the war on terror are the stuff of racism today. But these are not individual or random phenomena. Rather, they are components of an overall strategy that is unfolding in many Western post-immigration societies. The belief that immigration has reached its limits and that foreigners and Muslims are threatening our way of life used to be an argument of the right wing. But, as Arun Kundnani reminds us, it is now also being voiced by liberals and the center left. The consequence of this is that we are currently witnessing the return of the policy of assimilation. Packaged as "integration," the new assimilation sees multiculturalism as being "out of control" and racism as the fault of "too much diversity." Understanding the new assimilation is the key to understanding the challenges that racism poses today.

The new assimilation is conceived in response to the specific problems faced by the West in the post-9/11 age. However, while these problems – international terrorism, civil unrest, and the insecurity they breed – are clearly political in origin, the response to them is defiantly depoliticized. The clash of civilizations thesis sees culture and religion as the primary explanations of all global conflict. From this perspective, neither foreign invasion, nor economic globalization, nor systemic discrimination are the true culprits of the frustration that breed the terrorist response. The idea that there is a clash of cultures on a global scale, in contrast, is based on the belief that there is a fundamental and natural difference between Western and non-Western values. In order to rid the world of problems such as ethnic conflict and terrorism, this cultural, and indeed moral, clash must be overcome. For some it can only be overcome through conflict; for others it can be beaten by policy measures. The new assimilation is part of an overall tendency in politics, uniting left and right, to reduce everything to the moral and the cultural at the expense of the political or historical. It is a politics of gut reactions.

In short, the new assimilation responds to the belief that the problems of immigration and terrorism, but also gun crime, "race riots," and other problems seen as affecting minority communities, are due to "an excess of cultural diversity" (Kundnani 2007b: 29). The argument is simple: immigration societies have been too tolerant of minority cultures. Minorities have been allowed too much leeway to practice their own traditions at the expense of integration with the wider community. A whole host of events, from the murder of Dutch filmmaker Theo Van Gogh by a young Muslim in 2004, to the linguistic predominance of Spanish in areas of California, to the London July 7, 2005, bombings have been blamed on the same thing: too much diversity.

The debate about the *future of multiculturalism* in Western societies has quickly come on the back of the events of 9/11. Both the conservative right and sectors of the liberal intelligentsia are involved in a critique of multiculturalism as the idea responsible, in their eyes, for a host of societal problems from terrorism to crime and violence.

At the core of the argument against multiculturalism is the belief that it has led minority groups to believe that they had the right to special treatment. Factors such as speaking languages like Spanish, Turkish, or Bengali at home instead of the language of the "host" country, or the prevalence of ghetto-like neighborhoods, are seen as the negative outcomes of multiculturalism. David Goodhart, the editor of *Prospect* magazine, in an article entitled "Too Diverse," argued that it is to be expected that those belonging to the dominant culture should fail to have solidarity with others who share none of their cultural heritage or values, especially when being asked to pay – in the form of taxation – for their presence in society. The issue of values is crucial because the argument against diversity is not only that culture creates irreparable divisions between people, but also that those with different cultures have incompatible values. There are "good" values and "bad" values. The latter, such as those of radical "Islamists" or of black single mothers, are seen as contributing to the destruction of "race relations" and the increase in social tensions.

The arguments against multiculturalism are based on two false assumptions. Firstly, they assume that multiculturalism has been instigated by minority groups against the interests of the majority. While the interpretation of multiculturalism differs from place to place, multicultural policy was construed in reaction to the politicization of blacks and ethnic minorities on the streets of cities like Los Angeles and London. The emphasis on culture replaced a political understanding of the link between poverty and racialization that motivated groups such as the Black Panther Party.

The belief today that multiculturalism is responsible for mistrust between communities and breeds homegrown terrorists is the paradoxical result of multicultural policies themselves. As a policy, multiculturalism results in the tendency to see minority groups as homogeneous and to reduce them to the fact of their cultural difference alone. Quite simply, while members of the dominant group in society are seen as having complex and differentiated identities, minorities are often seen as one-dimensional. Despite the multi-dimensional nature of the characters of all human beings – for example, the fact of being a woman, being educated, being gay or straight, or believing in God or being an atheist – very often we see those we conceive of as being different to us only in terms of their culture. As a result there is a common failure to recognize that within minority communities there is a huge range of opinions on religion, politics, sexuality, human rights, and so on, just as there is among the majority. The homogenizing tendency of multiculturalism has itself led to the idea that there are fundamental differences between cultural groups.

It is therefore crucial to distinguish between multicultural policy and multiculturalism as reality, or what some call "multiculturality." Multiculturalism is a fact of life in post-immigration cosmopolitan societies. It is a fact that many of us now live among a variety of people with origins from around the globe. What is being critiqued by those who wish an end to multiculturalism is not the policy but the *reality* of diversity. The attack on multiculturalism is an attack on the idea that diversity represents a richness. Instead, echoing arguments only voiced by the extreme right wing in the past, governments today commonly promote the idea that too much diversity is in itself a dangerous thing.

Furthermore, not only is it argued that immigration must be stopped in the interests of fighting racism, too much diversity itself is seen as a *cause* of racism. While, until recently, those who vote for extreme right parties were commonly condemned, mainstream politicians today claim to understand these voters. The belief that indigenous culture is being eroded by multiculturalism is, it is claimed, leading to an understandable increase in racism. According to such a view, racism is a normal reaction to the frustrations caused by what is portrayed as a veritable invasion by alien culture, in particular, in the current climate, Islam. The problem of racism is therefore being reduced to one of culture rather than politics. If cultural incompatibility and an excess of diversity are seen as the real causes of racism, it is no longer necessary for the complex political and economic factors behind migration or terrorism to be explained.

The new assimilation is a response to the perceived failures of multiculturalism and the challenges posed by "too much diversity," in particular the assumed cultural incompatibility of Islam with a Western way of life. Rather than directly opposing racism, *integration and the creation of social cohesion* are now portrayed as the means of bringing about intercultural understanding and ending racial discrimination. Three factors in particular illustrate the status quo on racism as we near the end of the first decade of the twenty-first century: the focus on integration/assimilation; the return of national values as the foundations for cohesion; and the emphasis on diversity and discrimination over multiculturalism and anti-racism.

First, the attack on multiculturalism, as we have seen, has given way to a focus on integration. Arun Kundnani (2007b: 24) defines what he calls "integrationism" as based on an "anti-Muslim political culture associated with the 'war on terror' in which the focus is on 'self-segregation,' alien values and forced assimilation." A red thread links the terrorist attacks in New York and London to the perceived failure of "race relations" in the West. The politics of gut reactions links complex and disparate phenomena – terrorism, gun crime, segregation, etc. – together and puts them down to the failure to create cohesive integrated societies. In order to resolve what is portrayed as the dissolution of our societies, it is vital that the question of integration be addressed. This is being done in two ways: by curbing unsolicited immigration and by developing programs for enhancing integration.

What does integration mean in practice? In Britain, riots that took place in 2001 led to the introduction of the idea of community cohesion. The population of the towns where the rioting took place was split down the middle: whites on one side, and South Asians on the other. They were leading parallel lives. Community cohesion aims at redressing these problems by developing schemes to bring members of different communities together, for example schoolchildren, for meetings in youth clubs or community centers. This approach is based on the return of the belief, largely discredited by the 1980s, that the problem of racism is due to a lack of intercultural knowledge. The more people from different groups get to know each other, the lesser the tendency towards prejudice and misunderstanding. However, the community cohesion approach sees both sides as equally responsible for prejudice and thus fails to take into account the role of institutional racism and white privilege.

The failure of integration is seen, not only as the explanation for the breakdown in communication between different groups in society, but also as a measure of crime and delinquency. For example, a French report published in 2004 proposed that delinquency is the result of failed integration. It noted that children as young as three years of age whose parents do not speak to them in French can display tendencies towards delinquent behavior. The report recommended that mothers "of foreign origin should be obliged to speak in French to their children at home so that French becomes the only language they use to express themselves." As Saïd Bouamama, the sociologist who cites this example, remarks, the failure to integrate is therefore seen as the sole responsibility of parents rather than of the state or wider society. Clearly, the association between failed integration and delinquency from early childhood adds to creating the stereotype of "immigrants" as the main culprits of crime.

Of course, creating cohesive communities is not itself a negative objective. Yet two problems in particular beset ideas such as cohesion and integration. First, to be effective, cohesion cannot be achieved without the recognition that communities can only be built through trust and not through coercion. In the current climate, the principal problem facing the task of integration is the premise that the breakdown in community relations is due to the alien ways of minority communities and the threat they pose to a justifiably suspicious indigenous population. Thus, rather than working on what white and non-white communities have in common, community cohesion is predicated on a culture of one-sided blame. Second, integration is clearly assimilation by another name: it is not that all members of society are being asked to integrate into a shared vision of what the society of the future should be. Rather, "integration" requires assimilation into a set of preordained national values that often fail to incorporate the extent to which Western societies have been transformed by desegregation and immigration.

Advocates of community cohesion emphasize that integration should involve a commitment to the values of the society, values that are not seen as the outcome of cultural intermixture, but of the national heritage of the country. The assumption is that the national values of the USA, Australia, or the Netherlands are more valuable than those of immigrants' countries of origin. In particular, the values stressed are those such as tolerance, fairness, equality, and liberty. Rather than being universal, these values are seen to be particular to Western nations and their people.

The constant linking of values to the dual themes of immigration and terrorism raises important questions of who these values are for. National values in the West are constructed in opposition to what are assumed to be the uncivilized values of the Other. They are reactive rather than proactive, based on an assumption of the corrupting influence of outsiders rather than on the fact that a belief in simple common decency is not reserved for places like the USA or Europe, but is the way most people wish to live. What turns individuals to crime or violence is not different values bred by alien cultures, but subordination and rejection. These, sadly, are universal experiences, not exclusive to "minorities" and "foreigners."

In conclusion, where does the current climate leave the fight against racism? Under the new assimilation rubric that imposes national values in the aim of integrating – and civilizing – the Other, racism itself has been repackaged. Racism has lost its meaning as a specific idea based on the essentialization of the Other as inferior: racialization. It has become a two-way process. "Reverse racism" against local populations under attack by alien cultures is now seen as being as, if not more, significant than the racism this book details. Two transformations in the way racism is talked about are the fundamental outcomes of this changing interpretation of racism and they have significant effects for the ongoing attempt to resist it.

First, racism has been repackaged as "discrimination." The specific history of racism, its connection with the complex histories of nationalism, colonialism, slavery, and immigration has thus been eroded. The tendency to talk about discrimination or about a general violation of human rights is part of an attempt to see racism on an equal plane with other forms of injustice. While the consequences of discrimination on the grounds of physical ability, gender, or sexuality for example are no less serious than racism, they do not have the same origins. Speaking about racism in terms of generalized discrimination belongs to the tendency of erasing the institutional and political roots of racism and to see it, once again, as little more than prejudice. The failure to deal with racism as a legacy of the evolution of certain states, in specific and context-dependent ways, makes it impossible to deal with it head-on. Racism will remain a fixture of our societies so long as it is nebulously portrayed as discrimination, prejudice, intolerance, or, as is increasingly the case, a justifiable fear of the unknown.

Related to the discourse of discrimination is diversity. Diversity has become a catch-all term for talking about the nature of post-colonial and immigration societies. The vagueness of the term leads to an ahistorical view of how our societies became diverse. Diversity is generally understood to be a code word for multiculturalism. However, from a legislative and policy perspective, diversity covers the gamut of "difference" from disability to sexual orientation to minority ethnicity. This is marked by the move away from avowed anti-racist campaigns towards pro-diversity activities. During 2006, the Council of Europe mounted a youth campaign for diversity and human rights under the slogan "All Different – All Equal." The message of its organizers was that to be *for diversity* was positive whereas to be *against racism* was negative and off-putting for potential supporters.

The attractiveness of the idea of diversity is that it evokes difference. In our postmodern consumerist societies, we all want to feel a little different, and thus a bit unique. Diversity helps achieve this by making difference non-specific. No one wants to be branded an outsider, so talking about diversity serves to sell a vision of society as excitingly eclectic, a rich tapestry of uniquenesses. The flipside of this attractive image is that the vague idea of diversity allows us into the comfort zone where those who are *too diverse* can be conveniently forgotten. Diversity implies a confined and recognizable space: it is curry and cous cous but not hungry and destitute asylum seekers; it is bangles and ankle chains but not *hijabs*.

While these examples may seem like semantic squabbles, they are representative of the current tendency by governments, international organizations, and consequently the general public, to turn a blind eye to the specificity of racism, and indeed all forms of discrimination. This specificity is bound up in the history of racism that is also, as this book has aimed to demonstrate, the history of the modern Western world. Any attempt to understand the contemporary political phenomena of terrorism, migration, and globalization will be assisted by gaining insight into why racism in our societies persists. An engagement with this history will also help us to go beyond it. As Frantz Fanon, a man whose life was finally given over to the struggle against racist domination and whose analysis of racism is so fundamental to our understanding, wrote:

> It is through the effort to recapture the self and to scrutinize the self, it is through the lasting tension of their freedom that men will be able to create the ideal conditions of existence for a human world. (Fanon 1986: 231)

Glossary

antisemitism Prejudice and discrimination against and/or persecution of Jews.

apartheid The policy of strict racial segregation and discrimination against people of color in South Africa from 1948 to 1994.

caste Any exclusive and restrictive social or occupational class or group; rigid class distinction based upon birth, wealth, etc., and operating as a social system or principle.

colonialism The system or policy by which a country maintains foreign colonies, especially in order to exploit them economically.

cosmopolitanism A way of thinking and living that is not bound by local or national habits and prejudices, that partakes of many parts of the world.

degeneracy The state of being deteriorated, corrupted, depraved; having been reduced from a formerly superior condition.

demography The statistical science dealing with the distribution, density, and vital statistics of populations.

diversity Demonstrating or including variety and difference.

Enlightenment An eighteenth-century European philosophical movement characterized by rationalism, a quest for learning, and a spirit of skepticism and the drawing of conclusions through direct observation in social and political thought.

ethnicity One's ethnic classification, affiliation, or identity, often defined by customs, characteristics, language, common history, etc.

eugenics A movement devoted to improving the human species through the control of hereditary factors in mating.

genocide The systematic killing of, or a program of action intended to destroy, a whole national or ethnic group.

historicism A theory of history that states that the course of events is determined by unchangeable laws or cyclical patterns.

imperialism The policy and practice of forming and maintaining an empire in seeking to control raw materials and world markets by the conquest of other countries and the establishment of colonies; the policy and practice of seeking to dominate the economic or political affairs of underdeveloped areas or weaker countries.

Jim Crow Discrimination against or segregation of African-Americans in the pre-Civil Rights era of the United States.

nationalism Devotion to one's nation; patriotism; excessive, narrow, or chauvinistic patriotism.

naturalism A theory of ethics that states that distinctions between good and bad can be reduced to factual terms and statements according to the dictates of psychology, biology, etc.

phenomenon Any fact, circumstance, or experience that is apparent to the senses and that can be scientifically described or appraised; any extraordinary thing or occurrence.

racialization The claiming of racial differences in character, intelligence, behavior, etc.; the assertion of one race's superiority over others and the attempt to maintain the "purity" of that race.

Romanticism An eighteenth- and nineteenth-century movement that revolted against neoclassicism and was characterized in literature, music, and art by freedom of form and spirit, an emphasis on feeling and originality, and a sympathetic interest in primitive nature, Medievalism, Orientalism, and the "common man."

Social Darwinism A term that references Charles Darwin's theories of natural selection and evolution, applying them to human society. The term often refers to the notion of "survival of the fittest," social evolution through natural selection, and eugenics. Darwin himself never ascribed to any of these notions.

For more information

American-Arab Anti-Discrimination Committee (ADC)
1732 Wisconsin Avenue NW
Washington, DC 20007
(202) 244-2990
Web site: http://www.adc.org
The ADC is a civil rights organization committed to defending the
rights of people of Arab descent and promoting their rich cultural heritage. The ADC, which is nonprofit, nonsectarian, and
nonpartisan, is the largest Arab-American grassroots organization
in the United States. It was founded in 1980 by former U.S.
Senator James Abourezk and has chapters nationwide. The ADC
is at the forefront in combating defamation and negative stereotyping of Arab-Americans in the media and wherever else it is
practiced.

Anti-Defamation League (ADL)
Department: RL
P.O. Box 96226
Washington, DC 20090-6226
Web site: http://www.adl.org
The Anti-Defamation League was founded in 1913 "to stop the
defamation of the Jewish people and to secure justice and fair
treatment to all." Now the nation's premier civil rights/human relations agency, the ADL fights anti-Semitism and all forms of big-
otry, defends democratic ideals and protects civil rights for all. A
leader in the development of materials, programs and services, the
ADL builds bridges of communication, understanding and respect
among diverse groups, carrying out its mission through a network of thirty regional and satellite offices in the United States
and abroad.

Do Something, Inc.
24-32 Union Square East, 4th Floor
New York, NY 10003
(212) 254-2390, ext. 236
Web site: http://www.dosomething.org
Do Something believes teenagers and young people everywhere can improve their communities. It leverages communications technologies to enable teens to convert their ideas and energy into action. Its aim is to inspire, empower, and celebrate a generation of doers: young people who recognize the need to do something, believe in their ability to get it done, and then take action.

Gay & Lesbian Alliance Against Discrimination (GLAAD)
104 West 29th Street, 4th Floor
New York, NY 10001
(212) 629-3322
Web site: http://www.glaad.org
GLAAD empowers real people to share their stories, holds the media accountable for the words and images they present, and helps grassroots organizations communicate effectively. By ensuring that the stories of lesbian, gay, bisexual, and transsexual people are heard through the media, GLAAD promotes understanding, increases acceptance, and advances equality.

Human Rights Watch (HRW)
350 Fifth Avenue, 34th Floor
New York, NY 10118-3299
(212) 290-4700
Web site: http://www.hrw.org
The Human Rights Watch is dedicated to protecting the human rights of people around the world. It stands with victims and activists to prevent discrimination, to uphold political freedom, to protect people from inhumane conduct in wartime, and to bring of-fenders to justice. It investigates and exposes human rights violations and holds abusers accountable. The HRW challenges governments and those who hold power to end abusive practices and respect international human rights law. It enlists the public

and the international community to support the cause of human rights for all.

National Association for the Advancement of Colored People (NAACP)
National Headquarters
4805 Mt. Hope Drive
Baltimore MD 21215
(877) NAACP-98 [622-2798]
Web site: http://www.naacp.org
The mission of the National Association for the Advancement of Colored People is to ensure the political, educational, social, and economic equality of rights of all persons and to eliminate racial hatred and racial discrimination. The vision of the NAACP is to ensure a society in which all individuals have equal rights and there is no racial hatred or racial discrimination.

National Organization for Women (NOW)
100 H Street NW, 3rd floor
Washington, DC 20005
(202) 628-8669
Web site: http://www.now.org
Since its founding in 1966, NOW's goal has been to take action to bring about equality for all women. NOW works to eliminate discrimination and harassment in the workplace, schools, the justice system, and all other sectors of society; end all forms of violence against women; eradicate racism, sexism, and homophobia; and promote equality and justice in society.

U.S. Equal Employment Opportunity Commission (EEOC)
131 M Street, NE
Washington, DC 20507
(202) 663-4900
Web site: http://www.eeoc.gov
The U.S. Equal Employment Opportunity Commission is responsible for enforcing federal laws that make it illegal to discriminate against a job applicant or an employee because of the person's race, color, religion, sex (including pregnancy), national origin, age (40 or older),

disability, or genetic information. The EEOC has the authority to investigate charges of discrimination against employers who are covered by the law.

Web Sites

Due to the changing nature of Internet links, Rosen Publishing has developed an online list of Web sites related to the subject of this book. This site is updated regularly. Please use this link to access the list:

http://www.rosenlinks.com/ciss/race

For further reading

Introduction

Balibar, Etienne and Immanuel Wallerstein. 1991. *Race, Nation, Class: Ambiguous Identities*. London: Verso

Hall, Stuart. 1980. "Race, Articulation, and Societies Structured in Dominance," *Sociological Theories: Race and Colonialism*. Paris: UNESCO

Hannaford, Ivan. 1996. *Race: The History of an Idea in the West*. Baltimore: Johns Hopkins University Press

MacMaster, Neil. 2001. *Racism in Europe 1870–2000*. Houndmills: Palgrave

Wieviorka, Michel. 1994. "Ethnicity and Action." In John Rex and Beatrice Drury, eds, *Ethnic Mobilisation in a Multi-cultural Europe*. Aldershot: Avebury

Chapter 1

Balibar, Etienne. 1994. *Masses, Classes, Ideas: Studies on politics and philosophy before and after Marx*. New York: Routledge (chapter 8)

Balibar, Etienne and Immanuel Wallerstein. 1991. *Race, Nation, Class: Ambiguous Identities*. London: Verso (chapters 3 and 12)

Dikotter, Frank. 1992. *The Discourse of Race in Modern China*. Stanford, CA: Stanford University Press

Du Bois, W.E.B. 1946. "Colonies and Moral Responsibility," *Journal of Negro Education*, 15, no. 3: 311–18

Foucault, Michel. 2003. *Society Must be Defended: Lectures at the College de France, 1975–1976*. London: Picador (chapters 3 and 4)

Gellner, Ernest. 1983. *Nations and Nationalism*. Oxford: Blackwell

Gobineau, Arthur comte de. 1915. *The Inequality of the Human Races*. Trans. Adrian Collins. New York: G.P. Putnam & Sons

Goldberg, David Theo. 2002. *The Racial State*. Malden, MA and Oxford: Blackwell

Hall, Stuart. 1997a. *Representation: Cultural Representations and Signifying Practices*. London: Sage

Hannaford, Ivan. 1996. *Race: The History of an Idea in the West*. Baltimore: Johns Hopkins University Press (chapters 7, 8, and 10)

Hesse, Barnor. 2007. "Racialized Modernity: An analytics of white mythologies," *Ethnic and Racial Studies,* 30(4): 343–63

Hobsbawm, Eric and Ranger, Terence, eds. 1983. *The Invention of Tradition.*
Cambridge: Cambridge University Press

Knox, Robert. 1969 [1850]. *The Races of Men: A Fragment.* Miami:
Mnemosyne ed.

MacMaster, Neil. 2001. *Racism in Europe 1870–2000.* Houndmills: Palgrave
(Introduction and chapters 1 and 2)

Nicholson, Philip Yale. 1999. *Who Do We Think We Are? Race and Nation in the
Modern World.* New York: Armonk and London: M.E. Sharpe

Noiriel, Gérard. 1991. *La Tyrannie du National: Le droit d'asile en Europe, 1793–
1993.* Paris: Calmann-Lévy

Smith, Anthony D. 1986. *The Ethnic Origins of Nations.* Oxford: Blackwell

Voegelin, Eric. 1933a [2000]. *Race and State.* Trans. Ruth Heim. Baton Rouge
and London: Louisiana State University Press

Chapter 2

Appiah, Anthony. 1985. "The Uncompleted Argument: Du Bois and the Illusion
of Race." *Critical Inquiry* 12(1), "Race," Writing, and Difference: 21–37

Barot, Rohit and Bird, John. 2001. "Racialization: The genealogy and critique
of a concept." *Ethnic and Racial Studies* 24(4): 601–18

Boskin, Joseph and Dorinson, Joseph. 1985. "Ethnic Humor: Subversion and
Survival." *American Quarterly* 37(1), Special Issue: American Humor: 81–97

Douglas, Mary. 1970. *Natural Symbols: Explorations in Cosmology.* London: Barrie
and Rockliff, Cresset Press

Du Bois, W.E.B. 1903. *The Souls of Black Folk.* Chicago: A.C. McClurg & Co.

——. 1940. *Dusk of Dawn: An essay towards an autobiography of a race concept.*
New York: Harcourt

Fanon, Frantz. 1986. *Black Skin, White Masks.* London: Pluto Press

——. 2001. *The Wretched of the Earth.* London: Penguin Classics

Gilroy, Paul. 1987. *"There Ain't No Black in the Union Jack": The cultural politics
of race and nation.* London: Unwin Hyman

Goldberg, David Theo. 2006a. "Racial Europeanization," *Ethnic and Racial
Studies* 29(2): 331–64

Hall, Stuart. 1997a. *Representation: Cultural Representations and Signifying Practices.*
London: Sage

——. 1997b. *Race, the floating signifier.* Media Educational Foundation

Herrnstein, Richard J. and Murray, Charles. 1994. *The Bell Curve: Intelligence and
Class Structure in American Life.* New York: Free Press

hooks, bell. 1995. *Killing Rage, Ending Racism*. London: Penguin

Lévi-Strauss, Claude. 1975. "Race and History." In *Race, Science and Society*. New York: Whiteside and Morrow, for UNESCO

Macey, David. 2000. *Frantz Fanon: A Life*. London: Granta Books

Nelson, Vednita. 1993. "Prostitution: Where Racism and Sexism Intersect," *Michigan Journal of Gender & Law* 1: 81–9.

Williams, Patricia J. 2000. "Race and Rights." In Les Back and John Solomos, eds, *Theories of Race and Racism: A Reader*. London: Routledge

Young, Robert, J.C. 1995. *Colonial Desire: Hybridity in Theory, Culture and Race*. London: Routledge, 1995

Chapter 3

Arendt, Hannah. 1966. *The Origins of Totalitarianism*. New York & London: Harcourt Brace Jovanovich

Avnery, Uri. 2003. "Manufacturing Anti-Semites." In Alexander Cockburn and Jeffrey St. Clair, eds, *The Politics of Anti-Semitism*. Petrolia CA: Counterpunch

Bauman, Zygmunt. 1989. *Modernity and the Holocaust*. Cambridge: Polity Press

Handelman, Scott. 2003. "Trivializing Jew Hatred." In Alexander Cockburn and Jeffrey St. Clair, eds, *The Politics of Anti-Semitism*. Petrolia CA: Counterpunch

Taguieff, Pierre-André. 2002. *La nouvelle judéophobie*. Paris: Milles et une nuits

Traverso, Enzo. 1996. *Pour une critique de la barbarie moderne: Ecrits sur l'histoire des Juifs et de l'antisémitisme*. Lausanne: Editions Page Deux

Chapter 4

Balibar, Etienne and Immanuel Wallerstein. 1991. *Race, Nation, Class: Ambiguous Identities*. London: Verso (chapter 1)

Barker, Martin. 1981. *The New Racism: Conservatives and the Ideology of the Tribe*. London: Junction Books

Carter, Robert. 2007. "Genes, genomes and genealogies: The return of scientific racism," *Ethnic and Racial Studies* 30(4): 546–56

Dawkins, Richard. 1976. *The Selfish Gene*. London: Oxford University Press

Gilroy, Paul. 2000. *Against Race: Imagining Political Culture beyond the Color Line*. Cambridge MA: Belknap

Goldberg, David Theo. 2002. *The Racial State*. Malden, MA and Oxford: Blackwell (chapter 8)

——. 2006b. "Deva-stating Disasters: Race in the Shadow(s) of New Orleans," *Du Bois Review* 3(1): 83–95

Hesse, Barnor. 1999. "'It's Your World': Discrepant M/multiculturalisms." In Phil Cohen, ed., *New Ethnicities, Old Racisms.* London: Zed Books

Schmidt, Peter. 2007. "At the elite colleges – dim white kids." *The Boston Globe,* 28 September (http://www.boston.com/news/ globe/editorial_ opinion/oped/articles/2007/09/28/at_the_elite_colleges___dim_ white_kids)

Sherman, Arloc. 2006. "African-American and Latino families face high rates of hardship." *Center on Budget and Policy Priorities,* 21 November 2006 (http://www.cbpp.org/11–21–06pov.htm)

Chapter 5

Agamben, Giorgio. 2005. *State of Exception.* Trans. Kevin Attell. Chicago: University of Chicago Press

Bhattacharyya, Gargi. 2006. "War on Our Doorstep: Islamicizing 'race' and militarizing everyday life." In Alana Lentin and Ronit Lentin, eds, *Race and State.* Newcastle: Cambridge Scholars' Press

Bouamama, Saïd. 2005. "L'intégration contre l'égalité (Première partie), Les enseignements d'Abdelmalek Sayad," http://lmsi.net/

Cole, David. 2003. *Enemy Aliens: Double Standards and Constitutional Freedoms in the War on Terrorism.* New York: The New Press

Fekete, Liz. 2001. "The Emergence of Xeno-Racism," *Race and Class* 43(2): 23–40.

Goodhart, David. 2004. "Too Diverse?," *Prospect,* February

Huntington, Samuel P. 1996. *The Clash of Civilizations and the Remaking of World Order.* New York: Simon & Schuster

Kundnani, Arun. 2007a. *The End of Tolerance: Racism in 21ˢᵗ century Britain.* London: Pluto Press

Said, Edward. 1978. *Orientalism: Western Conceptions of the Orient.* London: Routledge

Sivanandan, A. 2007. "Racism, liberty and the war on terror"(The Global Context), *Race and Class* 48(4): 45–96

UNHCR. 2006. "Number of asylum seekers halved since 2001, says UNHCR," 17 March 2006 (http://www.unhcr.org/cgibin/texis/ vtx/news/opendoc.htm?tbl=NEWS&id=441a7d714)

Bibliography

Agamben, Giorgio. 2005. *State of Exception*. Trans. Kevin Attell. Chicago: University of Chicago Press

Appiah, Anthony. 1985. "The Uncompleted Argument: Du Bois and the Illusion of Race," *Critical Inquiry* 12(1), "Race," Writing, and Difference: 21–37.

Arendt, Hannah. 1966. *The Origins of Totalitarianism*. New York & London: Harcourt Brace Jovanovich

Avnery, Uri. 2003. "Manufacturing Anti-Semites." In Alexander Cockburn and Jeffrey St. Clair, eds, *The Politics of Anti-Semitism*. Petrolia CA: Counterpunch

Balibar, Etienne. 1994. *Masses, Classes, Ideas: Studies on politics and philosophy before and after Marx*. New York: Routledge

Balibar, Etienne and Immanuel Wallerstein. 1991. *Race, Nation, Class: Ambiguous Identities*. London: Verso

Barker, Martin. 1981. *The New Racism: Conservatives and the Ideology of the Tribe*. London: Junction Books

Barot, Rohit and Bird, John. 2001. "Racialization: The genealogy and critique of a concept." *Ethnic and Racial Studies* 24 (4): 601–18

Bauman, Zygmunt. 1989. *Modernity and the Holocaust*. Cambridge: Polity Press

——. 2003. *Wasted Lives: Modernity and its Outcasts*. London: Polity Press

Bhattacharyya, Gargi. 2006. "War on Our Doorstep: Islamicizing 'race' and militarizing everyday life." In Alana Lentin and Ronit Lentin, eds, *Race and State*. Newcastle: Cambridge Scholars' Press

Boskin, Joseph and Dorinson, Joseph. 1985. "Ethnic Humor: Subversion and Survival." *American Quarterly* 37(1), Special Issue: American Humor: 81–97

Bouamama, Saïd. 2005. "L'intégration contre l'égalité (Première partie), Les enseignements d'Abdelmalek Sayad," http://lmsi.net/

Bunyan, Tony. 2007. "Racism, liberty and the war on terror" (State Policies and programmes in the "war on terror'), *Race and Class* 48(4): 45–96

Carter, Robert. 2007. "Genes, genomes and genealogies: The return of scientific racism," *Ethnic and Racial Studies* 30(4): 546–56

Cole, David. 2003. *Enemy Aliens: Double standards and constitutional freedoms in the war on terrorism*. New York: The New Press

Dawkins, Richard. 1976. *The Selfish Gene*. London: Oxford University Press

Dikotter, Frank. 1992. *The Discourse of Race in Modern China*. Stanford, CA: Stanford University Press

Douglas, Mary. 1970. *Natural Symbols: Explorations in Cosmology*. London: Barrie and Rockliff, Cresset Press

Du Bois, W.E.B. 1903. *The Souls of Black Folk*. Chicago: A.C. McClurg & Co.

———. 1940. *Dusk of Dawn: An essay towards an autobiography of a race concept*. New York: Harcourt

———. 1946. "Colonies and Moral Responsibility." *Journal of Negro Education* 15(3): 311–18

Fanon, Frantz. 1986. *Black Skin, White Masks*. London: Pluto Press

———. 2001. *The Wretched of the Earth*. London: Penguin Classics

Fekete, Liz. 2001. "The Emergence of Xeno-Racism," *Race and Class* 43 (2): 23–40

Foucault, Michel. 2003. *Society Must be Defended: Lectures at the College de France, 1975–1976*. London: Picador

Gellner, Ernest. 1983. *Nations and Nationalism*. Oxford: Blackwell

Gilroy, Paul. 1987. *"There Ain't No Black in the Union Jack": The cultural politics of race and nation*. London: Unwin Hyman

———. 2000. *Against Race: Imagining Political Culture beyond the Color Line*. Cambridge MA: Belknap

Gobineau, Arthur comte de. 1915. *The Inequality of the Human Races*. Trans. Adrian Collins. New York: G.P. Putnam & Sons

Goldberg, David Theo. 1997. *Racial Subjects: Writing on Race in America*. New York and London: Routledge

———. 2002. *The Racial State*. Malden, MA and Oxford: Blackwell

———. 2006a. "Racial Europeanization," *Ethnic and Racial Studies* 29(2): 331–64

———. 2006a. "Deva-stating Disasters: Race in the Shadow(s) of New Orleans," *Du Bois Review* 3(1): 83–95

Goodhart, David. 2004. "Too Diverse?," *Prospect*, February: 30–37

Hall, Stuart. 1980. "Race, Articulation, and Societies Structured in Dominance." *Sociological Theories: Race and Colonialism*. Paris: UNESCO

———. 1997a. *Representation: Cultural Representations and Signifying Practices*. London: Sage.

———. 1997b. *Race, the floating signifier*. Media Educational Foundation

Handelman, Scott. 2003. "Trivializing Jew Hatred." In Alexander Cockburn and Jeffrey St. Clair, eds, *The Politics of Anti-Semitism*. Petrolia CA: Counterpunch

Hannaford, Ivan. 1996. *Race: The History of an Idea in the West*. Baltimore: Johns Hopkins University Press

Herrnstein, Richard J. and Murray, Charles. 1994. *The Bell Curve: Intelligence and class structure in American life*. New York: Free Press

Hesse, Barnor. 1999. "'It's Your World': Discrepant M/multiculturalisms." In Phil Cohen, ed., *New Ethnicities, Old Racisms*. London: Zed Books

——. 2007. "Racialized Modernity: An analytics of white mythologies." *Ethnic and Racial Studies* 30(4): 343–63.

Hobsbawm, Eric and Ranger, Terence, eds. 1983. *The Invention of Tradition*. Cambridge: Cambridge University Press

hooks, bell. 1995. *Killing Rage, Ending Racism*. London: Penguin

Huntington, Samuel P. 1996. *The Clash of Civilizations and the Remaking of World Order*. New York: Simon & Schuster

Kundnani, Arun. 2007a. *The End of Tolerance: Racism in 21st Century Britain*. London: Pluto Press

——. 2007b. "Integrationism: The politics of anti-Muslim racism." *Race and Class* 48(4): 24–44.

Lévi-Strauss, Claude. 1975. "Race and History." In *Race, Science and Society*. New York: Whiteside and Morrow, for UNESCO

Lorrain, Henri. 2002. "France – The Paris massacre of 17 October 1961," *Searchlight*, October

Macey, David. 2000. *Frantz Fanon: A Life*. London: Granta Books

MacMaster, Neil. 2001. *Racism in Europe 1870–2000*. Houndmills: Palgrave

Memmi, Albert. 1974. *The Colonizer and the Colonized*. London: Earthscan

Nelson, Vednita. 1993. "Prostitution: Where Racism and Sexism Intersect," *Michigan Journal of Gender & Law* 1: 81–9

Nicholson, Philip Yale. 1999. *Who Do We Think We Are? Race and nation in the modern world*. New York: Armonk and London: M.E. Sharpe

Noiriel, Gérard. 1991. *La Tyrannie du National: Le droit d'asile en Europe, 1793–1993*. Paris: Calmann-Lévy

Said, Edward. 1978. *Orientalism: Western conceptions of the Orient*. London: Routledge

Sivanandan, A. 2007. "Racism, liberty and the war on terror" (The Global Context), *Race and Class* 48(4): 45–96

Smith, Anthony D. 1986. *The Ethnic Origins of Nations*. Oxford: Blackwell

Taguieff, Pierre-André, ed. 1991. *Face au racisme 1: Les moyens d'agir*. Paris: La Découverte

——. 2002. *La nouvelle judéophobie*. Paris: Milles et une nuits

Traverso, Enzo. 1996. *Pour une critique de la barbarie moderne: Ecrits sur l'histoire des Juifs et de l'antisémitisme.* Lausanne: Editions Page Deux

Voegelin, Eric. 1933a. [2000]. *Race and State.* Trans. Ruth Heim. Baton Rouge and London: Louisiana State University Press

Wieviorka, Michel. 1994. "Ethnicity and Action." In John Rex and Beatrice Drury, eds, *Ethnic Mobilisation in a Multi-cultural Europe.* Aldershot: Avebury

Williams, Patricia J. 2000. "Race and Rights." In Les Back and John Solomos, eds, *Theories of Race and Racism: A Reader.* London: Routledge

Young, Robert, J.C. 1995. *Colonial desire: Hybridity in theory, culture and race.* London : Routledge, 1995

Index

About the Author

Alana Lentin is a lecturer in sociology at the University of Sussex. She is the author of *Racism and Anti-Racism in Europe* (2004).